SINGING AND IMAGINATION

Singing and Imagination

A *Human Approach to a*
Great Musical Tradition

THOMAS HEMSLEY

OXFORD
UNIVERSITY PRESS

OXFORD

Great Clarendon Street, Oxford OX2 6DP

Oxford University Press is a department of the University of Oxford.
It furthers the University's objective of excellence in research, scholarship,
and education by publishing worldwide in

Oxford New York

Athens Auckland Bangkok Bogotá Buenos Aires Cape Town
Chennai Dar es Salaam Delhi Florence Hong Kong Istanbul Karachi
Kolkata Kuala Lumpur Madrid Melbourne Mexico City Mumbai Nairobi
Paris São Paulo Shanghai Singapore Taipei Tokyo Toronto Warsaw

with associated companies in Berlin Ibadan

Oxford is a registered trade mark of Oxford University Press
in the UK and in certain other countries

Published in the United States
by Oxford University Press Inc., New York

© Thomas Hemsley 1998

British Library Cataloguing in Publication Data
Data available

Library of Congress Cataloging in Publication Data
Hemsley, Thomas.
Singing and imagination: a human approach to a great musical
tradition / Thomas Hemsley.
p. cm.
Includes bibliographical references (p. ••) and index.
1. Singing—Instruction and study.   2. Singing—Interpretation
(Phrasing, dynamics etc.)   I. Title.
MT892.H446 1998   783'04—dc21   97-21959
ISBN 0-19-879015-5
ISBN 0-19-879016-3 (pbk.)

5 7 9 10 8 6

Printed and bound in
Great Britain by
Biddles Ltd, Kings Lynn, Norfolk

Foreword

When Bruce Phillips approached me about writing a book on singing, I was at first rather apprehensive, thinking that there were already a confusing number of books on the subject, and that in any case singing was not really something that could be learned from books.

On further consideration though, I realised that the great majority of these books were not really about singing at all, but about voice, and that they were mostly manuals concerned primarily with the anatomy and physiology – the mechanics – of the vocal organs; instructions about how to produce the voice. Believing that the 'how' of singing is largely meaningless without first clearly establishing the 'why' and the 'what', and having observed in the course of my own experience with young singers that, given genuine talent, many of the difficulties they encountered originated quite simply in the lack of a sufficiently clear vision of what they were trying to achieve, I decided to write a book which might help young singers, and others interested in the art of singing, to a better understanding of what singing is all about; to help them ask meaningful questions as a necessary preliminary to finding meaningful answers; to focus, in fact, on the human and imaginative dimension, not as an optional extra, but as an essential prerequisite of the art of singing.

This book is dedicated to the teachers, coaches, conductors, directors, and composers from whom I have learned during half a century of singing; and to the fine singers whom I have been able to observe at close quarters, and with whom it has been my privilege to work in an exceptionally large and wide-ranging repertoire in the opera houses and concert halls of many countries. My thanks are also due to my son William for much helpful advice, and to my wife for her steady encouragement.

Contents

viii   *Contents*

List of Music Examples

PART I

General Introduction

In 1872 Charles Darwin published an interesting and rather neglected book, *The Expression of the Emotions in Man and Animals*. In it he writes: 'I have been led to infer that the progenitors of man probably uttered musical tones before they had acquired the powers of articulate speech.' Modern research supports Darwin, and shows that the vocal organs are indeed controlled by a more primitive part of the brain than that which controls speech.

Later he writes: 'When the voice is used under any strong emotion, it tends to assume, through the principle of association, a musical character.'

In the book he refers to a highly interesting essay by the philosopher Herbert Spencer, written in 1858, called 'The Origin and Function of Music'. Spencer writes: 'All music is originally vocal. All vocal sounds are produced by the agency of certain muscles. These muscles, in common with the body at large, are excited to contraction by pleasurable and painful feelings. Therefore it is that feelings demonstrate themselves in sounds as well as in movements.'

Spencer goes on to examine the different voice qualities which result from different feelings; the question of pitch and the allied question of intervals: in fact the various modifications of voice which lead to expressiveness. He writes:

These various modifications of voice become not only a language through which we understand the emotions of others, but also a means of exciting our sympathy with such emotions. Have we not here then adequate data for a theory of music? These vocal peculiarities which indicate excited feeling are those which especially distinguish song from ordinary speech.

And one further quotation:

If music, taking for its raw material the various modifications of voice which are the physiological results of excited feeling, if it intensifies combines and complicates them; if by carrying out these further, more consistently more unitedly and more sustainedly, it produces an idealised language of emotion, then its power over us becomes comprehensible. But in the absence of this theory, the expressiveness of music appears to be inexplicable.

Richard Wagner, in his essay 'About Conducting', wrote:

The human voice is the practical foundation of music, and however far
the latter may progress upon the path of its choice, the boldest expressions of the composer or the most daring bravura of the instrumental
virtuoso must always return to the essence of song for its ultimate
vindication.

If all these observations are true—and I find it hard to
believe that they can reasonably be questioned—then it is
easy to understand the article on singing by Deacon in the
first edition of the *Groves Dictionary*, which states:

As surely as singing—that is the Italian school of singing—is allowed to
die out, its decease will react upon instrumental music. Instrumental
music gets its legato and the more subtle parts of its phrasing from the
singer, while the singer owes his precision and more musicianly qualities
to the instrumentalist. The two branches help one another, and while
the vocalist acknowledges his obligation to the instrumentalist it is rank
ingratitude on the part of the instrumentalist not to be equally candid.
If persisted in, this ingratitude will be suicidal.

The concern—amounting to obsession—of much contemporary music with sound, or its debased form, noise, rather
than with human expressiveness; with pitch rather than harmony; the concern of singers with voice for its own sake,
rather than with 'modifications of voice' which provide a
'language of emotion', seems to me to be in danger of pushing
us unconsciously towards a form of 'suicidal ingratitude';
not, as suggested, for instrumentalists, but for singers themselves, who resort more and more to non-singing activities
such as exaggerated gesture, grimacing, and verbal caricature,
to replace the subtleties of vocal expression, while their actual
singing remains—often very competently, even beautifully—
bland, when not self-consciously brutal and ugly.

The human voice holds a very special place in the world of
music. The direct links between the world of sound and the
world of human experience are twofold: the human ear and
the human voice. The two are intimately related, not only by
association but by direct nervous connection. I am not
suggesting that music is simply a matter of voice and ear.

Music is, as Ernest Ansermet writes, 'a phenomenon of consciousness—an internal happening, an activity of feeling which manifests itself externally in musical images'. I am speaking of the raw material of this musical manifestation— the human voice—and the means by which it is perceived, and ultimately controlled—the human ear.

There are a great many possibilities for making vocal sounds. The scream, the shout, the moan, the bark, the hiccough are all produced by the vocal organs; but they are not, or have not been until recently, accepted as singing within the European tradition. Tibetan monks cultivate extraordinary deep vocal vibrations, which are said to be highly therapeutic, and to aid meditation. Mongolian shepherds cultivate two-voiced singing, which is no doubt a highly skilled accomplishment. Considering the lonely life of Mongolian shepherds it is probably very important for them to be able to sing duets with themselves. Within the tradition of European classical singing, where partners and human audiences are easy to come by, such accomplishments are superfluous.

The traditions of singing in countries of the Far East, and India, for example, are quite different from the European tradition. The folk-music singing traditions of the Balkan countries are very accomplished, but again are something different. I am not in any way dismissing, or belittling the value of, such traditions; but when I write of singing, I mean the solo singing of the European classical tradition, as it has developed since the Renaissance in Italy. Singing in this tradition has not been cultivated as an aid to meditation, nor has it been concerned with such oddities as two-voiced singing. It does not take as its starting-point the wish to make a sound, but the wish to express and to arouse all kinds of emotions through music.

This distinction is absolutely fundamental, involving as it does specialized (though totally natural) use of the voice. Just as the same muscles are used for walking and for running, but used in importantly different ways, so the same muscles are used in making a gentle moan and singing the role of the Queen of the Night in Mozart's opera *The Magic Flute*. The second is not (as some voice theoreticians would have us believe) an extension of the first. It is doing something significantly different with the same muscles; it also involves the use of muscles not primarily concerned with sound production. You cannot learn to be a successful sprinter by going for regular gentle walks; nor can you turn yourself from a stroller to a sprinter by studying anatomy and physiology. A gentle moan can be a helpful relaxation for the vocal muscles, but it is not singing as we understand it. In a similar way, patterns of breathing which are appropriate to meditation or relaxation are quite inappropriate to a vigorous activity (singing) which is primarily concerned with the expression of emotion. Indeed 'relaxation' is perhaps the most abused word in the singing studios of today. Expressions such as 'poise', 'alertness', 'tonicity', 'buoyancy' are more appropriate and also more accurate.

Lucie Manén in her book *Bel Canto* quotes the Italian singer and laryngologist Francesco Bennati, who wrote in 1832 of his observations that there are different mechanisms for voice production, one the normal speaking voice, which can also be used for singing, which he called *Voix ordinaire*, and another used by the great singers of his day, which he called *Voix orotonde*, and which she calls 'ventricular mechanism'. This latter way of singing gives the greatest possibilities for the modulation that is necessary for the subtleties of artistic singing. The best and most concise description of the difference that I know is to be found in Manén's book. Any investigation into singing which fails to recognize the different ways in which the voice can be used can be in the end very confusing and misleading for both singers and teachers.

I am constantly disturbed by the current tendency to separate what is called 'technique' from what is called 'interpretation'. This is a concept which comes from the instrumental branch of music. In the case of singing these two things cannot be separated, for the simple reason that the only thing that stimulates the voice to action is the urge to express something; in particular, to give expression to thoughts and feelings through music. The whole object of learning to sing is to improve the connection between the emotional, poetic, and musical impulses, and the body, which responds by producing appropriate sound. It is a process demanding patience and total dedication, in which a good teacher can be of the greatest help, and the wrong teacher can do untold damage. It is a process in which the initiative must always be taken by singers themselves.

Perhaps the first prompting to write this book came to me as a result of a conversation I had with a professor of singing at the end of some master-classes that I had given. The conversation was more or less as follows:

PROFESSOR. Thank you very much for your work with our students. But I see that you do not teach technique at all, only interpretation.

T.H. Do you find that any of the students were actually singing better at the end than they were at the beginning?

PROFESSOR. Oh yes! I would say that most of them were singing better—some of them much better.

T.H. You mean actually better, vocally.

PROFESSOR. Certainly.

T.H. That is what I call technique.

What I suppose the professor had meant was that I had not taught anatomy; I had in fact spent three days encouraging the young singers to use their imaginations, to be clear about their intentions, and to try to forget their obsessive preoccupation with muscular functioning—sometimes with dramatic results.

Let me be quite clear. I am not belittling the importance of technique—on the contrary, a well-established technique is essential. I am not suggesting that anyone can sing if his musical and emotional intentions are sufficiently strong. Although there are specially gifted individuals for whom that is undoubtedly true, for the vast majority it is a very dangerous notion. I am suggesting that frequently, what people understand by the word technique can be misleading, or even counter-productive. Technique in singing as we understand it is, or should be, a matter of learning how to mobilize, strengthen, and refine the impulse to express emotions and thoughts through vocal sound; to improve the connection between the imagination and that vocal sound, and to communicate what arises from music and poetry. This cannot be done if the vocal activity is separated from that impulse.

Lamperti, one of the great teachers of the classical Italian way of singing in the nineteenth century, writing to his pupil William Earl Brown, maintained: 'There is no 'bel canto' system of teaching. Mental, physical and emotional reactions are the fundamentals of this old school.' The important word here is 'reactions'.

The study of singing, in our tradition, can be reduced to two things:

1. Training the mind and the imagination to give clear and precise impulses to which the body can react.
2. Training the body to react with maximum precision and energy.

These two aspects are inseparable; any attempt to separate them can only result in singing which is not appropriate to the highest aims and ideals of European classical song.

My first singing teacher, Arthur Cranmer, always insisted that in the main, singing was an exercise of the mind and not of the body. He frequently reminded his pupils 'Be sure never to let anything come out of your mouth unless it has passed through your mind.' Lamperti said something very similar a hundred years earlier: 'It is through our desires, our sensations, our perceptions that we gain control of our activities in body and mind. This is especially true of singing. Our acts are fashioned by our ideals of melody, harmony and poetry.'

Of course there are physical aspects to singing which must be trained; it would be foolish to deny that. Singers must be physically fit; they must be free of blockages in their breathing; they must cultivate a good kinaesthetic sense, and a posture appropriate to the vigorous act of singing, but which does not produce unhealthy muscular tensions. They must learn to be aware of, and use, different resonances. They must be well centred, and must develop a clear awareness of the point of concentration from which their singing is directed. They must have a strong feeling for the life-force within them, and they must be able to distinguish between that and mere personal excitement. Above all they must posess an instinct for music—a talent for singing. Imagination alone is not enough, and to sing with uncontrolled emotion spells disaster. But every time a student makes a vocal sound which is not guided by the imagination, and which is devoid of *élan vital* and emotional content, he is separating singing from its source, and therefore conditioning himself to make vocal sounds which are not appropriate to singing within our best tradition. To quote Sir Charles Santley, the most famous English singer of the second half of the last century, later a renowned teacher (after describing the simplest possible basic vocal exercise): 'Give your artistic feelings full play even at this early stage; a simple scale or a single note may be interesting if sung with the feeling of an artiste.'

I myself was trained as a scientist, and am the last person to decry science. But science is only useful when it is appropriate. The 'science' which seeks to reduce everything to a mechanical model is not appropriate to the human activity of singing. Indeed the wisdom of earlier 'pre-scientific' days is sometimes more truly scientific than some of the 'explanations' propounded by teachers who, lacking personal experience of singing, or more than superficial understanding of true scientific principles, substitute half-digested scientific jargon for true understanding: more truly scientific, because it was concerned with the science—knowledge—of human feelings and emotions. An understanding of anatomy and physiology, if accurate, can be of help to teachers in dealing with singers' problems; but too much concern with anatomy, and the purely mechanical, anatomical aspects of singing on the part of singers, can actually inhibit their ability to sing. Indeed, frequently, this over-concern with anatomy can be the cause of those very problems.

Many research programmes are undertaken into the functioning of the larynx. They are, without doubt, of importance to science, to the medical profession, and to medical voice therapists, but mostly their results are not helpful to those studying the art of singing. Indeed, by effectively encouraging the idea of singing as a purely physical, instrumental, activity, and by their devotion to a particular generally accepted mechanical model for the singing voice, they can often be a serious hindrance.

Some years ago I attended an international congress of voice experts in New York. Learned scientists read papers about all manner of aspects of anatomy, physiology, and acoustics. Frequently they played recordings of the voices which had been analysed in the course of the research. In every single case my reaction was: 'But that is not singing.' I formed the impression that a high proportion of research into the human voice has been undertaken to analyse the vocal activity of people who could not sing; certainly who could not sing in what is generally recognized as the European classical tradition. One particular 'voice guru', a medical man turned singing teacher, stood up and said with great passion that it was time we got rid of the 'pernicious notion of beautiful singing', and concentrated entirely on the concept of the correctly functioning larynx. I subsequently read an article by him, in which he stated that all voices, particularly those of 'so-called natural talents' were in need of therapy. There are singers with a divine gift of song, whose voices are balanced and responsive. Their singing in all its aspects can be improved by careful training, and artistic guidance; but they are not in need of therapy. They need, as an insurance policy, to acquire more and more awareness of what they are doing; but just as a healthy person can easily be made sick by unnecessary medical treatment, so a fine natural singer can be injured by tuition which seeks to change, rather than to confirm, the delicate natural balance of the singing voice.

Such natural talents should not be looked upon with suspicion, as oddities, or as candidates for therapy, but as models. Much more attention should be paid to observing just what it is that contributes to such talent.

The great English tenor of the last century, Sims Reeves, in his admirable short book *The Art of Singing* states: 'Singers should not purposely study the anatomical conditions of the throat and lungs; it is with the emotional, not the anatomical side of his art that the singer has to do. For the practical purposes of singing, a knowledge of the muscles of the throat is as useless as a knowledge of the muscles of the arm is for the playing of cricket.' The physical aspect should be very simple; simple but infinitely precise and subtle in its application. Or as the Russian Sergei Levjik wrote: 'What constitutes vocal technique is in itself very little, but its details are amazingly varied in light of an individual's needs.'

Until the time of Manuel García junior, books about singing were concerned with training through carefully graded musical exercises, with a few simple hints about purely physical matters. Great emphasis was also placed on training the ear. García junior was a failed singer. He was the son of Rossini's tenor who was also an important composer and impresario and a great teacher. His sisters, Maria Malibran and Pauline Viardot, were two of the greatest prima donnas of the day. He quite understandably wanted to find out why his voice had failed, and he invented the laryngoscope, believing that it would help him if he could see what was happening in his throat. The laryngoscope was of great benefit to the medical profession, but not directly to singers, unless they were sick. First, use of the laryngoscope involves complete distortion of the delicate balance necessary for singing. It is possible to make vocal sounds while the laryngoscope is in use, but they are not the vocal sounds of good artistic singing; it therefore led to some serious misunderstandings about the act of singing. (It has to be said that modern techniques, though apparently an improvement in this respect, can be equally misleading.) Secondly, living in a time when anything that claimed to be scientific was given exaggerated respect, he was to a high degree responsible for turning the teaching of singing from an artistic to a scientific (all too frequently pseudo-scientific) exercise. The idea grew that singing could be taught in a purely instrumental way—by learning to make mechanically produced noises, and then adding musical meaning afterwards. This may or may not be true of other instruments, but if singing in the European classical tradition has its basis in the response to feeling, if the impulse which results in singing is the wish to express emotion through musical sounds, then any vocal activity which separates singing from this source must be of a different order, and from our point of view counter-productive. The human singing voice is not an instrument on which music is played; it is in its very nature an instrument of music. Hope for future scientific understanding of singing must surely be in the realm, not of anatomy, but of psychology, neurology, and the workings of the brain.

In defence of García himself, rather than of those of his disciples who climbed on to the fashionable 'scientific' bandwagon, I would like to quote Sir Charles Santley again:

Manuel Garcia is held up as the pioneer of scientific teachers of singing. He was—but he taught singing, not surgery ! . . . in all the conversations I had with him, I never heard him say a word about larynx or pharynx, glottis, or any other organ used in the production and emission of voice. . . . he used his knowledge for his own direction, not to make a parade of it before his pupils, as he knew it would only serve to mystify them, and could serve no good purpose in acquiring a knowledge of the art of singing. My experience tells me that the less pupils know about the construction of the vocal organs the better.

I am not for a moment suggesting that what Santley wrote was untrue. But I do suggest that the above passage indicates that García had more sense than to talk about such things to a man who was acknowledged to be one of the greatest singers of his generation.

In 1950, together with my friend Bernard Keefe, I visited John Mewburn Levien, a very alert and sprightly nonagenarian. He had been a friend of Santley, and disciple of García, in whose defence he had written many articles. In the course of our conversation, he said that he thought García was a great artistic personality, and a wonderful vocal coach, but that he never seemed to have any success with beginners, because his explanations about the mechanics of singing seemed to confuse and mislead them. In fact he was dismissed from his post at the Royal Academy of Music, partly because of internal politics, but chiefly, Levien admitted, because his young pupils did so badly.

It seems to me that for basically healthy singers, the anatomy that really matters is not the anatomy studied by the medical profession, but the anatomy of 'how it feels': the 'as if' anatomy. Everyone knows, to take a simple example, that the act of singing takes place during the expiratory cycle of breathing. Most good singers of my experience, however, describe the feeling of 'drinking in air' or 'continuing to inhale' while they are singing; a physical impossibility, but a strong and widely experienced sensation. As soon as a singer becomes aware of exhaling while singing, the quality of tone, and his ability to modulate, and to sustain long musical phrases is seriously diminished.

In *The Republic*, Plato defined music as consisting of three things: words, harmony, and rhythm. (It is interesting to note that, according to the Sufi master Hazrat Khan, the Sanskrit root-word for music, *sangita,* has three aspects—language, play, and movement.) My reading of this simple statement in the context of song interpretation is:

Words express thoughts. Under the heading '**Words**', therefore, I include:
> Text and diction.
> Musical form, phrasing, and prosody.
> Everything concerned with the intellectual content of a song.
> The singer's intention.
> In modern terms, I suppose one might say that by 'words', Plato referred to 'left-brain activity'.

'**Harmony**' is the language of feeling and emotion and includes:
> The harmonic contents of the song.
> Everything which affects the colour or timbre of the voice: mood, atmosphere, emotion, and vocal quality.
> Those things guided by intuition.
> 'Right-brain activity'.

'**Rhythm**' is all that gives life and energy to the song, and includes:
    The pulse of the song, accent, rhythm.
    The magnetism, and communicative powers of the singer.
    The 'gut feelings' of the impulse to express yourself.

Perhaps the talents which first lead people to want to sing, or even to devote their lives to the art of singing, come under the heading of 'Harmony'; a strong impulse to express feelings through musical sounds. But unless this is harnessed to 'words' it will never become art, and unless these two are strongly energized, the artist will never become a performer. Words, harmony, and rhythm—or head, heart, and guts—must all be part of the art of singing. Words and harmony must be there in equal, balanced proportion: rhythm, or the life-energy, must be there all the time.

This book then is not concerned with medical matters, nor with anatomy and physiology. It is not a book designed specifically to help those with vocal problems, except in so far that I believe a high proportion of vocal problems to have their origin in the mental attitude of the singer, and are frequently caused by obsessive concern with voice, and vocal mechanics, rather than singing and music. It is not, to use a motoring metaphor, a 'garage manual', but a book about 'driving'. It is not primarily concerned with methods of training, but perhaps will be of help in making the aims of training more clear. I do not concern myself with what are termed 'extended vocal techniques', because they are not a part of the tradition of singing about which I am writing; and also because their cultivation can too easily prove to be dangerously incompatible with the balanced fine-tuning which this tradition demands. It is a deliberately traditional approach to singing, and for that reason most of the sources I have quoted are from earlier times. Modern knowledge is of great value when appropriate; but it is necessary continually to assess its value with a critical eye, and to be suspicious of unquestioning acceptance of everything which is couched in scientific language, particularly if it leads to the rejection, rather than a clearer understanding, of what is of proven value. My early training as a physicist taught me always to look for what we used to call 'first principles'; perhaps this is my attempt to establish what those principles are.

This book is addressed to those with a gift for singing who would like to understand better how to approach putting that gift to use. It is not my intention to provide answers, still less to proclaim a method; but to help singers to ask meaningful questions. Singers must find their own inner impulse; the best teaching cannot provide that, and young singers should never depend on teachers, accompanists, or conductors to provide it for them. Teachers can, indeed must, stimulate the imagination of their students, but cannot provide it if it is lacking. As Tosi wrote in 1723: 'Whoever accustoms himself to have Things put into his Mouth, will have no Invention, and becomes a Slave to Memory.' Teachers must be aware of, and draw attention to, bad habits, but must not cause their pupils to become obsessed with them. Most bad habits can be traced back to a failing in the basic principles, in particular a failure of posture, intention, and imagination. If teaching is not to be merely palliative, teachers' first duty must be to understand these principles, and to inculcate them. Most singers need a teacher whom they can trust, who *must* be someone who knows what it feels like to sing, and to sing well. In the end, the only true teacher is the singer himself.

I believe that it is important to have a clear idea of what you wish to do or say before doing or saying it; so my plan is to try to define the things that a singer should aim for in terms of Plato's three categories, and to give some simple hints about how to go about achieving those aims.

PART II
The Basic Principles

Readiness to Sing:
The Raw Material

> Oh! How great a master is the heart! Confess it, my beloved singers, and gratefully own, that you would not have arrived at the highest Rank of the Profession if you had not been its pupils; own, that in a few lessons from it, you learned the most beautiful expressions, the most refined taste, the most noble action, and the most exquisite graces: own (even though it may seem incredible) that the heart corrects the defects of nature, since it softens the voice that is harsh, betters an indifferent one, and perfects a good one: own that when the heart sings you cannot dissemble, nor has truth a greater power of persuading: and, finally, make it known (for I cannot teach it), that from the heart alone you have learned that certain indescribable charm which runs softly through all the veins and finally reaches the very soul. Although the way to the heart is long and rugged, and known only to a few, a studious application will, notwithstanding, master all difficulties.
> (Tosi, *Observations on the Florid Song* (1723))

The 'heart' of which Tosi writes is not something imposed upon a mechanically produced vocal sound; it is, or should be, the very source of that sound.

The raw material of solo singing in our best classical European tradition, ever since the Renaissance, is 'the expression of emotion in sound; the body's reaction to internal and external stimuli in which the whole system participates' (L. Manén). This raw material is essential, and must be mined; but if it is to be turned into art, it must be developed, balanced, refined, and brought under the control of the singer's higher faculties.

Let us consider briefly, and as simply as possible, what happens when we sing:

1. An event occurs either in the surrounding environment or in the imagination of the singer;
2. The singer reacts to this event by tensing certain muscles, as a result of which;
3. A sound issues from the singer's mouth.

This sound is the end-result. The chain of events *must* start at the beginning.

As Sir Charles Santley wrote in his book *The Art of Singing* (1908): '*What is called* "Production" cannot be taught without teaching singing, and *vice versa.*' Or as Reynaldo Hahn has written: 'It is impossible completely to separate the physical realisation of singing from the inner forces that direct and control it.'

There is one important difference between singing and the playing of a musical instrument; a difference which should always be borne in mind. The playing of any musical instrument begins as a conscious act, initiated, it seems, in the left brain. A pianist must know that in order to make a sound he must press a key on the piano; that to make a sound of a higher pitch, the hand must be moved to the right, and so on. This involves doing something which is basically 'unnatural', and learning to do it in such a way as to make it 'second nature'—making voluntary actions seem like reflex actions—switching them over to the right brain, the right brain being that part which deals with instinctive, emotional, intuitive activity. In the case of singing, on the other hand, we are concerned with the opposite process: we are performing natural, instinctive, intuitive, reflex, 'natural' actions, and learning to refine and control them; to make them conscious and voluntary.

Any form of training which forgets this essential difference, which tries to train the voice as if it were an instrument, an object to be played upon, must result in a form of singing which, divorced from its emotional origins, cannot have the same direct emotional appeal. The voice is the singer; it should never be thought of as in any way separate from the singer.

It is, of course, perfectly possible to treat the voice instrumentally—to make vocal sounds which do not have their source in emotion, and to use these sounds for musical purposes. But such vocalization is, I suggest, not part of the best post-Renaissance European tradition of solo singing. The difference is not simply one of emphasis or style; it is fundamental.

In his study of Caccini's vocal technique, Professor David Galliver writes:

The singer of the sixteenth century had been essentially a consort singer, his aim to blend with his ensemble; with sweetness and beauty of tone he had achieved a mastery of the technique of florid singing. The meetings of the Camerata however heralded the current change of taste from consort singer to soloist. . . . No longer was music to be pure sweetness—it was to purge men of their passions not by soothing them, but by arousing in them those very passions. Singing was to use different vocal qualities to depict different emotions and effects. . . . In thus prescribing for singing vocal phenomena which they had observed in rhetoric and drama, theorists—albeit unknowingly—were highlighting the most significant characteristic of the voice, its power to express different emotions in different shades of vocal timbre, thus activating a whole system of primitive human reflexes. Used in this manner as a spectrum of human emotion the singing voice could reflect in characteristic colour and dynamic flexibility the variety of range and intensity of human moods, employing a quality which distinguishes singing from instrumental playing, where tone has a less direct origin.

The principle described above, which came to be known as 'cantare con affetto', was discussed in the preface to Caccini's *Le nuove musiche* (1602), was developed by Monteverdi and others, and marked a milestone in European vocal music. It has formed the basis for solo singing in the classical tradition—essentially the Italian tradition—ever since, except for recurrent periods in history when singers have temporarily lost contact with the source, and have become obsessed with the purely instrumental, and the more superficial, aspects of their art.

The impulse to sing, then, in our tradition, is not simply the wish to make a sweet sound, or a loud sound—or indeed to 'make' any sort of sound; it is the overwhelming urge to express feelings, to release emotions through vocal sound and through music, and then to share those feelings and emotions; to communicate.

More and more, it would seem, that today singers are concerned with the production of a preconceived sound, often taken from a recording—itself artificially adjusted to be as close as possible to a generally accepted, international, bland, easily recorded sound—rather than permitting the sound of their voice to be the result of the body's reaction to the workings of internal feelings, imagination, and the higher human faculties. Adjustments and 'improvements' are attempted at the purely physical, mechanical level, rather than at the level of the imagination and the intention. In the process, individuality and spontaneity are lost, and the direct connection between the musical sound, and human experience—something unique to singing as it has developed in our culture—is broken.

Singing involves an influx of vitality and energy which is an essential element in the expression of emotion. This vital energy is often appropriately referred to as the 'breath of life'. Bergson called it *l'élan vital*; the Hindus call it *prana*; the Chinese call it *chi*; in old Italian, the word *fiato* (breath) had this meaning in addition to its more prosaic one. It is this vital breath, not a bellows full of wind, that is the true source of vocal sound. If it is to be transformed into art, this energy must be consciously channelled; the energy must become sound. For the purposes of the art of interpretation, though, we should consider not just 'voice', or 'vocal sound', but 'modifications of voice'; because it is these modifications of voice, directly resulting from variations of feeling and mood and character, that turn vocal sounds into music—which distinguish 'singing' from mere vocalization.

Developing this impulse, tapping this energy, while maintaining the poise necessary for freedom of expression is, or should be, one of the first duties of any teacher of singing. In practice, anyone with a genuine gift for singing will have felt it strongly at some time, usually triggered by a sense of tremendous well-being; that moment when singing suddenly is the easiest and most natural thing in the world—the moment of feeling perfectly balanced, full of life, and free. It is possible, but unlikely, that someone who has never experienced this overwhelming need to sing may acquire it, but it is I believe fair to say that all those with a natural gift for singing will have felt it strongly at some time. It is in fact the strength of this joyful impulse which usually leads people to sing in the first place. Without it, the chances of achieving any degree of excellence as a solo singer are virtually nonexistent.

It is necessary for anyone aspiring to be a solo singer to have a talent for singing—just as it is necessary to have a talent for painting or dancing or chess. The posession of a strong or beautiful voice does not necessarily indicate such talent, or an instinct for singing. Voice is of course important, but its importance is, strictly speaking, secondary. What is of primary importance is for the voice to be capable of expressing everything which is contained in the music. The impulse to express oneself in song—the talent for singing—is an absolute essential. I know of many cases where vocal quality has been improved, within natural physical limitations, by careful study and training; but I personally know of no case where someone lacking a genuine talent for singing and for music has succeeded in singing really well, however sonorous their voice, however great their determination, ambition, and will-power.

Too many young singers, aspiring to a professional solo career, suffer under the delusion that a study of vocal mechanics will somehow enable them to acquire something which is not inherent in them—what nature has failed to provide for them—the gift of song. Too many teachers make a good living by encouraging such delusions. A talent for singing that has been badly mishandled can occasionally be released, and sufficiently developed to make a professional solo career, or fulfilling amateur activity, possible. But this occasional teaching success does not imply that singing talent is universal.

On the other hand, I must record that for every such talent that I have seen released, I can point to several young singers whose genuine instinct for singing, whose divine gift of song, has been dragged down to earth and spoiled by obsessive and misguided concern with vocal mechanics.

If the raw material of our singing is the expression of emotion, depending on the 'life-energy' of which I have spoken, then a singer's first task must be to find a way of mobilizing this energy. Any vocal sounds coming from the throat which do not have their source in this life-energy are not the sounds of singing as I understand it. Every time singers make such sounds, they are conditioning themselves to the production of mere vocal noises, useless for the art of interpretation of solo vocal music in our best tradition.

It is easy to recognize this energy when we see it in action. We see it in Olympic gymnasts or figure-skaters as they prepare for their routine. We watch them on our television screens as they establish their balanced posture, as they concentrate on the task ahead of them, as they gather their physical and mental energies, and as, after a moment of intense stillness and then an internal up-beat, they release them into controlled activity. When this energy is present, and abundant, everything seems easy. For the singer, it expresses itself as an overwhelming need, desire, and readiness to sing.

Singers must learn to mobilize this energy without losing the mental and physical poise which is essential to being flexibly and vitally alert, and accurately responsive to the workings of their imagination. This is one of the first essentials of what is called 'technique'.

William Earl Brown quotes his teacher, Giovanni Battista Lamperti (1839–1910), as saying that the sensation of readiness to sing is:

Like that of a tight-rope-walker as he steps on the wire;
Like that of a swimmer as he trusts the support of the water;
Like that of the listener who hears a mysterious sound in the quiet of the night;
Like that of the archer the instant before he releases the arrow;
Like that of the orchestral conductor, with his baton poised; . . .

All these acts demand a potent vitality, conscious, accurate control of energy, and complete knowledge of the thing attempted.

In the case of singing, what is that 'thing attempted'? The purpose of this book is to try and help singers define this for themselves. One thing is certain: without a clear vision of the thing attempted, the chances of realizing it are very remote indeed. There have been many supremely talented singers who have had very hazy, or even quite erroneous, notions about how they sing, in a purely anatomical sense. But there have never been truly great singers who lacked a clear vision of what it was they were trying to do, in the poetic, musical, and dramatic sense; who lacked direct contact with their feelings, their intuition, and their imagination. In his preface to *Le nuove musiche* (1602) Caccini wrote: 'Many evils arise from the fact that the performer has not made himself quite master of that which he wishes to sing.'

Whether the singer is expressing violent emotion or the utmost calm, whether the feelings he is expressing are intensely tragic, hilariously comic, or deeply spiritual, he should feel that their expression is the most important thing he has done in his life up to that moment. To quote Lamperti again: 'Do not sing until you feel that you would die if you didn't.'

Thus the first important principle is this:

> The source and raw material of singing in our European classical tradition is the emotional exclamation and the energetic reaction of the whole person to feeling. This raw material must be both activated and guided by the imagination and the intuition of the singer.

Singing should never be separated from its source.

Posture

If good singing is, as I have suggested, always a reaction, then the first thing that a singer must acquire is the ability to be ready and able to react. This means above all to have a good posture—to be in a state of readiness.

It is perfectly possible to make vocal sounds without good physical poise, but the fine-tuning of strong and flexible response—the subtle modifications of voice that we call singing—are rendered virtually impossible. Good posture is not something simply to be switched on when singers enter their teacher's studio, or when they step on to the concert platform or the operatic stage. It must be habitual.

A high proportion of the exercises that singing teachers recommend to their pupils are in reality attempts to compensate for bad postural habits. These tricks themselves frequently result in tensions, which are then in their turn compensated for by new tricks, and so on *ad infinitum*. All this can well be avoided if good posture and poise are established at the very beginning. Habitual good posture is one of the chief attributes of so-called 'natural talents'.

Enter a crowded room, a reception at which guests from a wide range of professions and activities are present. You would probably be able to make a fairly accurate guess as to the general nature of the occupations of many of those present. This guess would be based of course partly on facial characteristics and the way people are dressed. But perhaps the strongest indication would be through body language— their posture, and the way they moved. Dancers who train their bodies virtually every day of their professional lives are very easy to recognize. The same applies to most successful athletes. It should be so in the case of singers, who should be recognizable, above all, by the carriage of the head, neck, and upper spine. If we are to be well balanced and alert—ready to react—it is essential to acquire habits of posture which permit this.

This cultivation of good postural habits is sometimes very difficult for young aspiring singers, who live at a time when they are continually exhorted to 'relax'. Gaetano Nava's instructions, 'The singer must in general choose a dignified attitude, avoiding any ungraceful or affected movements, such as are characteristic of persons of imperfect education and little taste', may sound very old-fashioned, but even so, it is essential for young singers to cultivate the physical poise of which Nava speaks (while ignoring his social prejudice). It has nothing whatever to do with stiffness, or pomposity, and is rendered impossible by inappropriate relaxation. The word 'relax' is surely one of the most abused words of our time, particularly in singing studios, where fashions tend to move from one extreme to the other. The fashion for exaggerated posture, which resulted in tension and stiffness, has given way to the belief that relaxation is the answer to all problems.

Tension is the result of lack of balance or poise. The cure for tension is not simply relaxation, but the recovery of poise. Misguided attempts to relax while singing (a very energetic activity) are probably, in the end, responsible for more vocal problems, more unhealthy tension, than any other source.

Nobody would deny that it is essential to be able to relax; relaxation is an essential preliminary to and concomitant of any efficient activity. The benefits of this ability are expounded in hundreds—probably thousands—of do-it-yourself books on self-improvement. Huge amounts of money are paid daily to therapists who teach relaxation. It is a very good source of income; because whenever people learn to relax without at the same time acquiring well-centred, well-grounded, balanced, postural habits, one can be sure that very soon they find it necessary to return. As Karlfried Graf von Dürckheim says in his book *Hara*, 'It is characteristic of our time that people look only for ways and means of achieving right relaxation without giving much thought to what is right tension.' This is particularly important for those who, like singers, are involved in physically and emotionally demanding pursuits. It is important, indeed essential, for them to be able to relax, to release muscles when they are not needed; but a sprinter who relaxed at the starting-block would fall on his nose. Singers who try simultaneously to sing—to express emotion, and to communicate it to an audience—and to relax, will suffer an equivalent disaster. What usually happens is that singers, because of lack of dynamic coordination, and forgetting that singing is an activity of the whole body and personality, come to rely solely upon the specific sound-producing muscles in the throat, with resulting vocal strain. The other frequent result is that singers who are not well grounded, who have not established strength in the loins, tense muscles in the midriff, in the region of the diaphragm, searching for something, anything, which gives a feeling of security, however illusory. In fact, by doing this, they are simply blocking the flow of energy, and denying to themselves any possibility of strong and flexible response.

Lamperti said: 'Because of co-ordinate action, which intrigues the whole personality, muscular effort and will-power seem in abeyance. This gives rise to a feeling of ease so insidious that a singer begins to rely on relaxation of mind and muscle—a quicksand that brings disaster.... Do not become rigid, but never relax.'

It is a matter of poise. Singing requires a great deal of energy; it is of great importance that this energy is not wasted, either by forcing, or by tension which results in a blocking of energy. Energy must always be appropriate to the task in hand; too much is as bad as too little. It is therefore vital for singers to be able to distinguish between the feeling of freedom that comes from poise and physical coordination, and relaxation; to distinguish between balanced alertness and rigidity, between tonicity and unhealthy tension.

There are immensely beneficial side-effects of this cultivation of good postural habits. They are not only essential for good singing, they are in the widest sense essential to good health. Bad postural habits result in poor breathing and general lack of vitality, both physical and mental. The frequency of back problems is one only-too-obvious sign of the prevalence of poor posture. (It must be said here that, as Dr Paul Sherwood has pointed out in his book *The Back and Beyond*, bad postural habits, and associated health problems, can also have their origin in back injuries, sometimes relatively minor, and usually quite forgotten—proper cases for therapy.)

One of the essential qualities needed by professional singers is that they should be physically robust and healthy. Both the act of singing and the demands of the professional life require it. For this too, good posture is of the utmost benefit. Good health as well as good singing depends on healthy breathing. Breathing is a natural process; the ability to breathe in different ways in response to different needs should be a natural process. But for this natural process to happen in an efficient and spontaneous manner, good posture is essential.

There are innumerable detailed descriptions of this good posture, which I would prefer to describe in the simplest non-technical terms as the state of surprised, poised, alertness.

Imagine that you are taking a walk in the woods on a beautiful spring day. Suddenly you hear a strange noise which surprises you. (You are surprised—*not* shocked.) You become very still, poised, alert. All your senses are awake. You listen intently; you test the air. You open the jaw as if preparing to drink. You raise your chest, and you gather strength into your lower belly. You prepare for action, and are ready to react in whatever way is appropriate when the source of the noise is revealed. Your whole body is balanced, still, controlled; ready to attack, to run away, or simply to rejoice at the unexpected appearance of a friend; you are ready to sing. Throughout the whole of your singing activity, this condition of readiness to react must be maintained. It is often called 'support'. I dislike the term, first because it can too easily suggest that the voice is an object, and secondly because the very notion of 'support' can suggest rigidity—blockage of energy—instead of maintained vitality and buoyancy. A preferable expression might be 'gird your loins'.

The feeling of strength which is essential to this maintained alertness pervades the whole body but is centred in the pelvic region and the lower belly, in the place called in Japanese *hara*, in Chinese the *tanden*. Cultivation of this strength is an essential element in all Eastern physical disciplines. Awareness of this centre is described in modern Western terms as 'being well grounded', or 'well centred'. This feeling of being centred has both physical and psychological aspects. Dr Samuel Johnson, in the eighteenth century, described people with this quality as having 'bottom'. It involves a strong feeling for the body's centre of gravity—approximately two inches below the navel. This centre of physical strength is lower than one at first imagines it to be; but once one becomes aware of it, there is no mistaking the feeling of well-balanced strength and calm that such awareness brings. It is not the same as the extreme tensing of the muscles around the midriff—the blockage of vital energy, which many singers cultivate under the mistaken notion that this 'supports the voice', whatever that may mean; with such tension, the body is not free to react—the very opposite of what good singing requires.

It is useless, worse than useless, for a young singer to hope to achieve this physical poise and feeling of strength in the body's centre by instruction from someone who has never had the personal experience of being themselves well grounded. As in so many aspects of singing, the difference between the real thing and a good imitation are subtle, but absolutely fundamental. Good posture adopted purely mechanically, unless it is directly associated with the human feelings to which it is appropriate, will not last, and will in the end only result in rigidity and tension. Also, if good posture is confined to the teacher's studio or the concert platform or the stage, it will take up too much of the singer's attention and become problematical rather than second nature.

Our second important general principle, therefore, is this:

> For good singing, it is essential to adopt the well-balanced alert posture of those who, with their entire being, wish to share their thoughts and feelings. This posture must be habitual.

Practical Hints

The purpose of good posture is to dispose the body in such a way as to permit maximum freedom and efficiency of action. The singer must be ready and able to react without losing poise.

The actual physical requirements for right posture for singing are really very simple. They are concerned with the two flexible sections of the back, the lumbar region and the neck, with the shoulders, and the jaw. It is necessary to give attention to these parts, perhaps because, as some believe, we are still not completely adjusted to our upright human posture. For the rest it is largely a matter of bodily awareness and mental attitude. If the singer lacks this awareness, no amount of anatomical description will help. It is not enough to put the body, mechanically, into a posture which imitates an alert condition if one lacks the associated feelings of genuine alertness, balance, and buoyancy.

The feeling of being well grounded and well centred has nothing to do with the pushing down which is often recommended to singers. Nor has it anything to do with sagging, with inappropriate relaxation. Still less has it to do with an exaggerated tightening and holding of the muscles around the midriff—that energy blockage which is a sure way of denying to the breathing apparatus the freedom it needs for efficient, strong, and flexible activity. It is something much more subtle, but also much more powerful; a feeling of strength in the body's centre in the lower belly and the pelvis, which allows freedom and flexibility, buoyancy, of everything above it.

Every physical aspect of singing, as indeed any physical activity, is helped by an awareness that all movements are initiated in the spine. Any exercise that increases the singer's awareness of his back is beneficial. The 'lengthening and widening' of the Alexander technique is of an enormous help to many singers.

This feeling for the back, and the correct adjustment of the neck, head, and chest, can be greatly helped if singers avoid the mental attitude of *telling* their audience about what they are saying—of pushing themselves towards them—and instead feel that they are *sharing* the experience with them; if they apply 'magnetism', mentally drawing the audience, or their partners on stage, to themselves rather than trying to importune. This feeling of sharing can often achieve posture improvements in moments, that otherwise may take long (and expensive) anatomical studies and special therapeutic exercises to acquire.

There are many ways to locate the position of the body's centre of gravity. One is to go to a grand piano, and prepare to lift it. In the moment of preparation before making the lifting effort, you will feel the centre of strength in the lower belly. The position of this centre is almost certainly lower than you expect.

One very helpful way for singers to find their centre of gravity is to take a sudden snap breath, as if suddenly surprised, to expand the back, to open the lower ribs, and to observe the reaction in the lower abdomen.

Try sitting in a chair, head in hands and elbows on knees; then take a deep breath, and observe how the lower ribs expand. Now stand, and try to make the same expansion without the assistance of taking in a deep breath; this is impossible without what I have described as 'girding the loins'.

Another simple but subtle way, is to walk a few steps up a staircase, turn, and walk down again, observing the adjustments of balance in the body's centre of gravity that are associated with the turn.

Any singer who has to travel, standing, in a crowded bus or train, can practise finding his centre. Suddenly he will find that it is no longer necessary to hold on. The body will adjust naturally to the movements of the train, without fear of falling over. This can only be achieved in a well-balanced posture, with a low centre of gravity. Neither pushing down nor sagging will help. Only a feeling of buoyancy above the waist together with firm strength in the centre of gravity will achieve it.

In all these ways, it is essential to preserve the feeling of lengthening the back and of lifting the upper torso out of the pelvis.

Once the feeling for the centre has been found, awareness of this centre as the source of energy should be practised. While walking, be conscious of moving the centre forward rather than concentrating on moving the feet. The more you practise awareness of the centre, the more you will find that the body acts as a whole, rather than as a series of parts. You will become aware of the flow of energies; you will find for yourself the combination of grounded security and energetic buoyancy which is the aim of good posture.

In all these activities, it is important to direct everything from the 'steering-wheel'—the point of concentration between your eyes. (See the section 'Practical Hints: The Head-Voice and the *Imposto*' in the chapter 'Intention, Impulse, and the Anacrusis', below.)

The simple physical adjustments are described in detail in Lucie Manén's book *Bel Canto*. Their essentials are:

the frontal part (of the pelvis) is moved inwards and upwards and the rear part moves easily downwards. This disposition gives the pelvis the correct position of relaxation, with the lower back stretched downwards; the whole body is then extended.

The singer obtains the correct position of the neck by stretching it as far back as possible backwards and upwards, moving the cervical vertebrae backwards.

The maximum space within the rib-cage is obtained by rotating the small joint between the shoulder-blades and the collar-bone. . . . the arms are turned in the shoulder-joints sideways and outwards. (Manén, *Bel Canto*)

When the balanced adjustment of the neck and head is correct, the head *rests* on the end of the spine, and the neck *rests* on its base between the shoulders; the muscles of the neck and the organs and muscles within the neck are without tension, and it is possible for the head to take any position without destroying the adjustment.

This last is important. The head can be free to move in any direction without disturbing the balance of the vocal organs so long as the head is moved from the very top of the spine, not together with the neck. One of the most common faults of young singers is the habit of pulling back the head with every inhalation. They suck in the air, instead of allowing it to 'fall into' their body. The lengthening of the neck should always be maintained while singing. If done correctly, it does not in any way prevent the free movement of the head from its pivot at the top of the spine.

Bad postural habits are not by any means always directly associated with singing. Some years ago, I held a visiting professorship in Copenhagen, and gave lessons to a group of young singers. Several of them had the habit of pulling back the head and tensing the back of their necks when inhaling. The others seemed to have no problem in this respect. I was intrigued to find an explanation. Copenhagen is a city where virtually everyone rides a bicycle. I asked all the pupils what sort of bicycles they rode. All those with the habit of pulling back the head rode bicycles with dropped handlebars. The others all had upright handlebars.

If this sounds very complicated, then I recommend to you the simple advice given to me by Arthur Cranmer: 'When singing, always feel your collar with the back of your neck.' This reminds me of the story of a fine, though vain, tenor in pre-War Germany who always wore a monocle hanging on a tape around his neck, with which he used to play in a most elegant manner. When asked by one of his pupils why he never put the monocle to his eye, he replied: 'Oh, I don't need it to see. But if I play with it, and give it an occasional little tug, it helps remind me to keep my neck in the best position for singing.' This 'best position' is not in any way stiff; it is a matter of maintaining the right relationship between head, neck, and upper spine.

The other movable part which is of great importance for singers is the jaw. The jaw is opened at the rear as if for the chewing motion—*not* the biting motion. The lower jaw hangs weightlessly, and parallel to the upper jaw, separated by about one finger's width. In this position it is possible to combine the maximum pharyngeal space with the maximum freedom of action for the lips and the front part of the tongue which is necessary for crisp clear diction. Excessive opening of the jaw at the front actually tends to diminish the pharyngeal resonating space, and produces tensions in the vocal muscles. It also makes clear diction impossible, as does the completely relaxed sagging jaw often recommended by teachers of singing, whose pupils are instantly recognizable in spite, sometimes, of their sonorous voices, by their inability to articulate words or modulate their vocal sound, and by their inability to sing and to interpret vocal music in any but the most generalized way. The answer is, as always, *balance*. The weight of the jaw should be exactly balanced by its supporting muscles. It is then free to move in all directions without distorting the voice, or inhibiting diction.

The position of the jaw is in fact that which occurs naturally when a well-balanced person has a sudden pleasant surprise. It is also achieved by practising a strong, calm, inner smile (a true inner smile—the smile of the Buddha—not a calculated, superficial imitation).

Olga Averino writes:

The position of the jaw is extremely important . . . it should not be 'dropped' . . . The desirable position can be formed by a deep inner smile bordering on the feeling of laughter. It is impossible to sustain a smile when the jaw is dropped. Dropping the jaw is usually an attempt to release a tension in the neck and the back of the tongue, which can be a serious obstacle to singing. On the other hand, the position of the jaw, when there is an inner smile, makes the crisp formation of words in the front of the mouth easy and natural while at the same time it relaxes the neck and the back of the tongue. This way of forming words—with the tip of the tongue and with live lips while keeping an inner smile—improves diction immediately. It eliminates unnecessary 'mouthing' and helps miraculously with the pronuciation of foreign languages.

The good posture that I have described need not in any way inhibit movement on the operatic stage. Such movement is largely achieved by movements of the limbs, which should be entirely free to move, without disturbing the balance or the relationship between head, neck, and upper spine. This is something that can be, and should be, practised at any moment in everyday life.

Watch an athletics race on your television screen, and observe how the very best runners move. Their legs and arms are moving quite freely, and their heads and bodies appear to be quite still, moving forward as if on wheels. Singers can learn much from watching top-class athletes in action.

Let me remind you of the second principle that I stated earlier:

> For good singing, a well-balanced, alert posture is essential. This good posture must be habitual.

I include here some further quotations from great teachers and singers of the past:

The singer must in general choose a dignified attitude, avoiding any ungraceful or affected movements . . . The singer therefore, if only to render the exercise of the voice freer and more easy, must above all hold the head high and upright, without making any unseemly motion with the shoulders, with the arms or any part of the body; a noble attitude must be maintained, and the vocalist should, especially during the lesson, and when anxious to be heard to the best advantage, sing standing, that the voice may be produced more easily. (Nava)

To sing well you must continually feel 'hollow-headed', 'full throated', 'broad-chested' and 'tight-waisted'.

Head, neck and torso form a drum-like elastic unit, feeling hollow down to the waist, the rest of the body solid. A constant buoyancy in head, neck and upper chest is essential to free tone production and good diction. Some have called this a 'fixed high chest', which is a misnomer. There is nothing muscular about it, and it is not stationary. *It results from a desire to pronounce well and to give sonority to the voice.* [My italics]

To retain the sensations, and continue the feeling of co-ordination of singing, without constricting the throat or stiffening the muscles of the body, marks the great singer. Many confuse this ease of united action with relaxation, because laborious effort ceases. (Lamperti)

Always (also when not singing) draw in the part of your abdomen below the navel, as well as the navel itself.

Put yourself into the physical and spiritual state of one who is going to dive from a great height into the sea, or is training for the

championship in running, jumping, and so forth. . . . keep your shoulder-blades in without getting tense, and hold your breath without
becoming cramped. (Franca)

Josef Schmidinger, in his book *Biodynamische Stimmbildung*, gives an amusing and apt description of a man riding
a bicycle, hands free:

With head and chest held high, and with upright body, he sits on the
saddle of his bicycle.

With legs somewhat spread, he presses evenly on the pedals.

By means of a gentle rotation of his hips he, as it were, frees his upper
body from all constriction, so that from this position he is able to steer
his bike.

Smiling and yawning, he feels a deep breath below his diaphragm,
which produces a feeling of physical well-being.

In this position he can enjoy his ride, and is also ready to sing.

The right practice of Hara requires first of all the discovery of a new
support for holding the body upright. The aspirant must find this
support in the lower part of the trunk. Until he does so, he is either
tense, wrenching himself upwards in order to stand, or slack, sagging
down completely if he does not forcibly hold himself up. Support from
the lower trunk, although most clearly felt in the belly, lies actually in
the whole trunk. So the whole trunk will gain in firmness as soon as the
belly is free and able to take weight from above, while the small of the
back will acquire a new vitality. . . .

The whole body finds itself in flexible equilibrium. The difference in
the tension of the neck is a special criterion of right posture. It is as if
secret power soared up lightly from below and culminated in the free
carriage of the head.

. . . As soon as he experiences and realises that this new intentionally
adopted posture gives him a different feeling of life and that it brings a
new inner attitude, he can, and indeed must, begin his work with this
new inner attitude. He must not only stand differently, but stand as a
different person for indeed the man who stays calmly in his body centre
is different from the one who either forcibly draws himself upwards or
weakly sags downwards. (Dürckheim)

The singing teacher Molloy in Robertson Davies's novel *A
Mixture of Frailties* clearly knew what he was about:

Feet a little apart. Let your neck go back as far as it will—no, don't
move it, *think* it and let it go back itself. Now, *think* your head forward
and up *without* losing the idea of your neck going back. Now you're

poised. Get the muhd [mood] now—this time it'll be joy. Think o' joy, and *feel* joy. Open your lungs and let joy pour in—no, don't suck breath, just let it go in by itself. Now with your muhd chosen, say 'Ah', and let me hear joy.—Christmas! D'you call *that* joy! Maybe that's the joy of an orphan mouse on a rainy monday, but I want the real living joy of a young girl with her health and strength. Again—Ah, your jaw's tense. Get your neck *free*; think it free, and your head forward and up, and your jaw *can't* tense. Come on, now, try again.

Impulse, Intention, and the Anacrusis

Impulse

I have already spoken about the raw material of singing in our tradition: the impulse to express feelings and emotions through vocal sound. It is not the same as the *wish* to sing—the feeling that many people have when listening to a great singer ('Oh! I would love to be able to do that'). It is something much more basic, much more instinctive, more directly linked to 'the primaeval sounds and exclamations, with which men express their inner feelings and reactions to impressions from the world around them' (Manén, *Bel Canto*). This primitive impulse, together with a high degree of vital energy, is the essential raw material of singing, and must be cultivated and strengthened; but if it is to be turned into art, it must be controlled and guided by the singer's conscious intention. If the physical attributes of the singer are such as to make the voice strong and of an appealing character, then so much the better.

The singing 'impulse' involves, as I have already stated, the cultivation of a state of alert readiness, of balanced tonicity. Music is a matter of vibration. A slack violin-string, or a slack drumhead, cannot vibrate. Nor can they vibrate if they are in some way restricted. This same principle applies also to the human body, to singing.

This leads me to what I believe can be one of the most helpful aids to good singing. If singers, as they are often exhorted to do, think of their bodies as 'bellows' for the blowing-out (albeit controlled) of air, their bodies cannot be in a state of alertness, and can never achieve the sort of controlled, flexible response which we recognize as singing in our best tradition. If on the other hand they can feel their bodies as vibrating instruments (like the body of a cello)

which must be activated, and set in vibration, then they have
already gone a long way towards achieving the sort of balanced animation of which I speak. The control of breathing
can then come naturally, in response to the singer's 'impulse'
and 'intention'.

Activating the impulse is essential for good singing, and
it is important that this state of energetic physical alertness
should never become blocked—must never become rigid.
This is one of the dangers of too much study of anatomy.
Singers can too easily fall into the habit of trying to reproduce
the purely anatomical aspects of this state, particularly if they
have an anatomical diagram in their mind's eye. An impulse
can be cultivated, and it can be maintained (it requires dedicated practice, and great powers of concentration), but it
cannot be held. If it is held in a purely physical way, it ceases
to be a true impulse; the true state of alertness is lost, and the
body can no longer respond to the promptings of the singer's
imagination.

It is essential for singers to be able to distinguish between
the singing impulse and a state of personal excitement. This
latter state cannot be controlled, and it cannot be used for
artistic puposes. The true singing impulse provides the potential energy that can be directed by the singer's intention. It is
available for the art of interpretation, rather than for mere
'self-expression', usually synonymous with 'self indulgence',
and invariably synonymous with 'bad taste'. The heart must
be warm, the body must react, but the head must remain cool.

The development of the impulse is something that can
never be learned from a book; all that I can do here is to make
a few suggestions. It is largely a matter of developing spontaneity and strength of reaction without becoming tense. All
singers must discover this for themselves, although teachers
can help to stimulate it; but there can be no stereotyped
method. If teachers are to be of any help, they must possess
it themselves; how otherwise than from personal experience
can they be in a position to recognize it, and distinguish
clearly, in a pupil, between the real thing and mere mechanical imitation?

Remember that everything I say assumes a well-grounded, buoyant posture. The impulse has its physical centre in the lower abdomen, in the body's centre of gravity; activating it is what I have called 'girding the loins'.

In her excellent short book *The Principles and Art of Singing*, Olga Averino writes about impulse:

This state of vitality can be stimulated. Individuals must each find the best way to stimulate impulse in themselves. For some people the best way is to go through physical exercises and raise the vitality of the body. Others are stimulated by something very beautiful—music, some special performance, poetry, or nature. Anything that will induce the wonderful mood of wanting to sing, is helpful. Once in the mood, you will recognise it. You will feel wonderful, both peaceful and alive, and your full concentration will be focussed on the music. I want to emphasise that this influx of vitality is not excitement. To be in a state of excitement is like riding a runaway horse. You are not in control. But with the influx of energy, one feels very peaceful and confident. . . . All your inner forces are gathered in a moment of intense concentration and then this energy is released into the performance.

It is perhaps best thought of as play. Lucie Manén, at the end of a lesson, was wont to say, in her sometimes idiosyncratic English: 'Now my dear, go away and play with yourself.' By which I took her to mean: go and experiment; experiment with your feelings and your reactions; find out how your body reacts to different situations, different moods, and learn to react spontaneously and freely without losing your poise. Then try to be aware of the physical sensations associated with different feelings, without the actual emotional involvement. This requires a very high degree of concentrated attention. Above all, as in all play, *use your imagination*. Remember, and relive that first moment when you experienced that overwhelming urge to sing out of sheer *joie de vivre*.

It is easiest to start with happy exclamations, simply because these spontaneous reactions should not in any way be associated with unhealthy tensions. Another most valuable exercise is to cultivate the sense of wonder; the feeling of awe; the sense of being in the presence of something infinitely

greater than oneself. These experiments should first be practised in private, so avoiding the temptation to give an imitation of the real thing for the benefit of any observer.

One of the things that most characterizes the true professional among singers is the ability, whatever the personal
feelings of the moment, to switch on the state of joyful
vitality, without becoming tense, without losing poise. It is no
good simply hoping to feel like singing when the time comes,
and depending perhaps on the conductor or accompanist, or
the audience's welcoming applause, to provide the necessary
'lift'. This activating of the impulse as a preliminary to singing
is something that all singers must learn to do for themselves,
every time they sing, whether they are practising in the pri-
vacy of their home or performing in public.

Once it has been recognized and developed, the best and
simplest way for singers to activate the impulse is to have
a clear mental picture of the poetic, dramatic, and musical
content of the phrases they intend to sing.

Dancers and acrobats make use of another method of
switching on this state of physical well-being and alertness.
They have traditionally been taught to smile while doing their
work. This is not simply a superficial smile aimed at present-
ing a pleasing appearance, and which rapidly deteriorates
into a fixed grin, which can be intensely irritating to an
audience. The genuine inner smile is a powerful instrument
for lifting the spirits, and for energizing, and at the same time
calming the body; preparing the dancer to dance, the athlete
to jump; for preparing the singer in every way for singing.
Cultivation of the inner smile is also in many traditions said
to be a powerful way of ensuring feelings of well-being, and
good health. The true inner smile starts with the eyes, and
from there can be directed through the whole body, releasing
tensions and energizing as it spreads. It should be practised,
until it becomes habitual.

Singing must always have its source in vitality, initiated by
the imagination. Once a singer has learned to stimulate this
vital influx of buoyant energy, those long sessions of 'vocalizing', of 'finding the voice' before a performance become quite

unnecessary. Such sessions of vocalization without vitality are enervating, and only serve to condition the singer to the habit of making meaningless vocal noises, rather than singing. Once mental and physical vitality are established (this can sometimes take some considerable time, and varies very much from person to person), once the body and mind are awake, once the big muscles that hold and move the body are alive, the body poised and buoyant, then the delicate muscles concerned specifically with the voice need very little time to warm up in readiness for singing.

Most singers have their own private ritual for becoming well grounded, for establishing the state of calm, and for switching on their vitality. A few minutes of physical warming up, and a couple of minutes 'pulling faces' at yourself in the make-up mirror, or the shaving mirror, to wake up the face and the eyes, are more valuable than long spells of trying to warm up the voice by singing badly, and struggling to make it better. Such rituals, though, are only really effective if they are entirely personal.

I repeat: a good teacher can recognize the results and can suggest possible approaches. But there is no escaping it—this is something that all singers must learn to do for themselves.

The Russian tenor and teacher Sergei Levik writes in his memoirs:

The tenor Balaskov, who successfully sang in Leningrad, recently told me of the occasion when he happened to visit one of Medvedyev's classes, saying that he would always remember his capacity to awaken spirituality in the singing of his pupils, and create heightened emotional awareness so that *many techniques were imparted as a natural consequence.* [*My italics*]

It is important, however, to remember that it is one thing to acquire habits quickly by imitation, and quite another to master and establish those habits on a long-term basis.

All this depends, I repeat, on singers' posture, and on their feeling for their centre of gravity—of being properly 'centred'—on their poise, coupled with a feeling of potential energy—on a strong feeling of buoyant expectancy. As Lamperti said: 'Until silence is pregnant with tone urgent to be born, you are only making vocal noises.' This potential energy, this impulse, this physical need to sing and to communicate, is essential. Without it, any notion of vocal freedom, freedom of the body's response, freedom to utilize vital energy, the freedom which enables singers to modulate and modify their voices in response to the finest shades of feeling and intention, is largely meaningless.

Intention

The impulse to express feelings and emotions through vocal sound is in the realm of instinctive, automatic, reactive behaviour—the realm of right-brain activity. It provides the essential raw material of singing, but on its own it cannot become art. The art of interpretation demands that this impulse be directed and controlled. Interpretation begins with the 'intention'—it is here that left-brain activity comes into play. The idea of singing a simple phrase, or even a single beautiful note is, or should be, already a matter of conscious musical 'intention'. To quote Sir Charles Santley:

A simple scale or a single note may be interesting if sung with the feeling of an artiste, while if blurted out in a commonplace style, it may cause your neighbours to entertain a desire to indict you as a nuisance.

It is the musical, poetic, and dramatic intention which gives form to the raw material provided by the impulse. A single tone or a simple phrase must be imagined in all its aspects before it can be sung. The pitch, the colour, the words, and the feelings associated with them which are to be expressed, the musical phrase in its entirety—all these things must be formed in the imagination. The actual sound produced is the result of all this imaginative activity and yet, paradoxically, it is important that singers, while hearing and observing, do not actively listen to themselves or concentrate on the sound that they believe themselves to be making. The actual sound is the end-result of the preliminary activity; by the time the sound issues forth it is too late to do anything about it. The singer must always be thinking forward in time, never backward;

concentration on the result of an action which has already taken place inhibits the ability to think ahead. One of the most frequently repeated pieces of advice given to singers over the years has been: 'Feel yourself sing—hear yourself sing—but do not listen to yourself sing.'

Singers, so long as the preparation in all its aspects has been done, must be prepared to trust their own reactions, and to be surprised by the actual sound that they create. If, and only if, all the preparatory work has been done, can the singer's intuition be free to play its part. The 'mere' singer can become a true, spontaneous, and creative artist.

The impulse, the potential energy, must be there, waiting to be activated and given direction by the intention. Without intention, the impulse is of little use as far as the art of interpretation is concerned. For this reason, much of singers' work can be performed silently. They should not begin to sing, until there is a clear picture in their mind of what they intend to communicate through singing. Tosi in 1723 wrote: 'Singing requires so strict an Application, that one must study with the Mind, when one cannot with the Voice.' A century and a half later, Lamperti wrote: 'When you are sentient from head to foot, and know your song, then you are ready to sing.' In our own day, Maria Callas, asked about the 'secrets' of her singing, once said, simply: 'I know the score.'

I am not suggesting for a moment that everything a singer does must be calculated in advance, although that is true for most aspects of a song. Spontaneity is essential in any performance; but spontaneity is only possible, and permissible, when all aspects of a song which can properly be prepared have been mastered.

Subtle, spontaneous changes of direction when driving a car can only be achieved through mastery of the steering-wheel; and it is through the singer's steering-wheel, the point of concentration located between and slightly above the eyes, the energy-centre known to Eastern tradition as the 'Brow Chakra' or 'Third Eye', that spontaneity of the imagination can be turned directly into appropriate modifications of sound. This energy centre is associated with the intuition, and on the physical level, the autonomic nervous system. (See the section 'Practical Hints: The Head-Voice and the *Imposto*', below.)

Just as a painter's visual imagination depends for its realization on the control of the point of the brush, so a singer's poetic, dramatic, and musical imagination, the ability to respond to all shades of feeling and meaning, depends for its realization on mastery of this point of concentration, which provides a complete control panel for the modification of voice—the act of singing.

I remember working with a young and very talented soprano who one day found this point of concentration, together with her true head-voice (dealt with in the following section). I asked the accompanist if she noticed a difference. Her reply was, I thought, very revealing: 'Her singing has suddenly become much more *engaging*.'

Another memory: of a young singer who used to attend my Lieder classes. I noticed that her singing had improved quite dramatically. I asked her what had happened. She replied: 'I suddenly realized, as a result of something you said a couple of weeks ago, that good singing is to a large extent a matter of finding a special sort of concentration. I think I have found it.' She had in fact discovered the secret of her intention. She never looked back.

It is my experience, that many faults of singing which, too often, are assumed to have an anatomical cause, and are dealt with therapeutically at this physical, material level, are in fact failures of concentration—failure of concentrated anticipation on the part of singers—failure of intention.

Every time singers go through the motions of practising singing in the classical manner of our tradition, without both impulse and intention being clearly established in response to the activity of the imagination, they are conditioning themselves to making mere vocal noises. (I am not of course referring to mothers' relaxed crooning to their babies. Any mother singing under such circumstances with the concentration necessary for communicating strong feelings to a large public, risks serious competition from any self-respecting baby!).

Our third important principle is this:

> Imagination, together with the intention, is an essential prerequisite of good singing, and not an optional extra.

The Anacrusis and the Start of the Tone

I maintain that the first and most important foundation is, how to start the voice in every register. Not only that the intonation be faultless, neither too high nor too low, but that thereby the quality of the tone be preserved. (Caccini)

From earliest times, writers on the subject of singing have laid great emphasis on this beginning: the start of the note. Lucie Manén has drawn attention to this, and argues convincingly that it is the most significant factor in distinguishing classical singing from what is simply a development of ordinary speech.

I have suggested that the sort of singing about which I am writing should always partake of the nature of a reaction. I have stressed the importance of singers maintaining the alert posture which makes reaction possible. I have pointed out that there are two important aspects of singing:

> the impulse, which provides the necessary energy, and
> the intention, which guides that energy.

These two elements should be combined in the moment of preparation for singing, in the musical up-beat or 'anacrusis'.

It is a well-known dictum among singers, teachers, and coaches that 'The character of a phrase is determined by the first note.' What is often forgotten is that the character of that first note, and consequently of the whole phrase, in all its aspects, is determined by the up-beat. That up-beat is an essential part of the music, and of dramatic expression; it should never be separated from the phrase which is to come. For a singer, the up-beat should involve everything necessary as a preparation for singing; to prepare the body to react, and to release into physical reality what has been conceived in the imagination. The act of musical and dramatic imagination must come before, not after, the physical up-beat, or the intake of breath. The timing of this up-beat is an essential element in uniting the impulse with the intention, in turning the urge to sing into art.

The sequence of events is as follows:

1. The impulse to sing expresses itself in physical alertness, and readiness to react.

2. The clear vision of what is to be sung results in a musical-dramatic up-beat, and a 'surprised' breath, in the character of the phrase to be sung.

3. The start of the note, controlled from the *imposto*, occurs at the end of the up-beat, while the breath is momentarily still. Lucie Manén describes this form of vocal attack as a 'click'. Lamperti expressed it: 'The energy to start a tone must come from the action of the vocal chords themselves, as they separate, not from the impact of the breath pushed against them.' (In fact it is not just the vocal chords, but the whole glottis.) The start of singing must be a *reaction,* a definite beginning—not simply drifting in with the music. This means that the singer must, with the anacrusis, give his body something to which it can react. (It is no accident that so many exercises for the vocal attack from 'pre-scientific' days began on the off-beat—a simple way of starting the note as a reaction, rather than as an explosion.)

4. The continuing of this particular vocal sound depends on maintaining the state of alertness, and avoiding pushing out air. This is often described as the feeling of 'continuing to inhale', or of 'drinking'. It is of great assistance if singers think of their bodies as vibrating instruments, rather than as a bellows.

I repeat what I have stated elsewhere in this book. By the time the sound issues from a singer's mouth, it is too late to determine what character that sound should have. The chain of events must begin at the beginning. Everything depends on the preparation; that preparation must be incorporated into the anacrusis, and of necessity be initiated in the singer's imagination—an essential prerequisite of singing, not an optional extra.

Practical Hints: The Head-Voice and the *Imposto*

The impulse, the gut feeling of wanting to sing, the urge to sing, has its physical centre of strength in the lower abdomen—the centre of gravity. It is the source of the singer's energy, the 'motor'. The intention has its centre in the point of concentration between, and slightly above the eyes, in what Lucie Manén calls the *imposto*; what in the Viennese school was called the *Hochgriff*, the high grip. It provides the singer's 'steering-wheel'. The *imposto* has anatomical and neurological aspects, but primarily it is the energy centre associated with intense concentration.

The centre of concentration, the *imposto,* is naturally activated when we are surprised and alerted; when with our whole being we are testing our environment—when we are concentratedly listening and looking and sniffing the air like a wild animal. This 'control panel' for singing is something recognized and frequently described by singers, but difficult or impossible to account for in terms of the mechanical model on which most scientific research has been based. Perhaps, one day, neurological research will help.

Anyone familiar with the oriental concept of the 'Chakras' will easily recognize that I am referring to the 'Brow Chakra'. It is associated with the intuition, and on the physical level, the autonomic nervous system.

The *imposto* acts as an alternative control mechanism for the larynx, and for the fine adjustments necessary for vocal modulation. It cannot be activated by attempts to 'push the sound' into the mask. It is a mechanism which initiates, and controls; not simply a reaction. Its position is difficult to locate, while singing, unless the nasal and pharyngeal spaces are first opened up, and head resonances developed.

It is highly unlikely that someone who has no personal

experience of the *imposto* would be able to recognize it in others, and therefore be of help in teaching its use. Indeed those who have never found it tend to deny its existence, supported by experiments, using apparatus which renders its application impossible (such as a tube containing a camera passed through the nose), which claim to 'prove' that it is a mere fantasy. Too often, they forget that singing involves coordinate action of all the parts, and that interference with any one of them will result in incorrect observations. However, for any singer who has activated the *imposto*, there is no mistaking it; with well-established *imposto* singers can be in control. Without it, it is difficult to give accurate direction and meaning to basic vocal exclamations; the interpretation of words and music will lack focus and precision; the intuition will have no means by which it can directly influence the workings of the voice in any but the most generalized way; the finer and more subtle parts of communication through singing are rendered impossible. Establishing accurate control of this 'steering-wheel' without losing contact with the 'motor' is one of the essential skills that a classical singer must learn.

In practice, if singers are to develop the ability to respond with accuracy and subtlety to all shades of feeling and meaning, guided by the *imposto*, the head-voice or *mezza voce* must be an essential ingredient in all their singing. (By *mezza voce* I understand either pure head-voice, or mixed voice with a strong preponderance of head-voice—the two terms are in practice virtually synonymous.)

As Sims Reeves wrote:

Mezza voce singing—that is, the use of the head voice instead of shouting the upper notes of the chest range—seems to be well-nigh a lost art. Yet *mezza voce* is one of the chief charms of what the Italians call the antique school. . . . To be able to paint a song with ease, the singer must have a perfect control of *mezza voce*; any attempt at graceful or emotional singing will otherwise be merely ridiculous vocal wobbling. The penalty of failing to cultivate *mezza voce* will be the speedy destruction of the voice; barking and shouting, which many persons mistake for a spirited and dramatic delivery, is the singer's road to ruin.

He then goes on to warn about the confusion between genuine head-voice and falsetto, a confusion which has been greatly exacerbated by the current misuse of the term 'head-voice' by modern falsettists, to describe their activity.

As the term implies, falsetto is a false voice . . . Any attempt to add vibration to falsetto will at once result in the production of nondescript tone of very bad quality. It is impossible to make a *crescendo* on a falsetto note—it may swell out a very little, but a full, genuine *crescendo* cannot be done. This fact will help the learner to distinguish between the head register and the falsetto.

(Perhaps I should at this point clarify what Sims Reeves means by the word 'crescendo'. The singing crescendo indicates not only an increase in intensity or loudness, but also a deepening and enriching of the tone, an expansion of the vocal quality, like an orchestral tutti, rather than like a single instrument simply playing louder. It is because of the impossibility of developing this crescendo homogeneously into a full mixed voice from a falsetto beginning, rather than from a properly placed head-voice, that so many writers on singing, from Caccini onwards, have discouraged or forbidden the use of falsetto. This crescendo, followed by a diminuendo, starting and finishing with a well-placed head-voice, and passing through all shades of colour, was known as *messa di voce*. It was considered an essential skill, and an essential element in expressiveness, for all singers. Without the concentrated guidance from the *imposto*, its execution is not possible.)

Karl Scheidemantel wrote: 'The thorough training of the placed head-voice in woman as well as in man is the indispensible condition of further development. (To meet every doubt I wish to point out explicitly that I do not mean the *falsetto* of male voices).'

Franziska Martienssen-Lohmann, in her famous book *Der Wissende Sänger* writes: 'Unfortunately there are singing teachers who cannot perceive the difference between falsetto and the male head-voice; and as a result of extended experiments with falsetto, they deprive young male singers of the ability to develop the high range and piano quality of the genuine head-voice.'

The pure head-voice, or *mezza voce*, is an important expressive element, and should always be available to the singer. The pure, unmixed chest-voice is very rarely required in classical singing, and then only briefly, for very special effects. Virtually all classical singing should have a mixture of the two, the proportions being infinitely variable. One thing is certain, and it would be possible to double the size of this book with quotations from distinguished singers and teachers affirming this: the head-voice must always be part of the mixture, and should always lead.

Sims Reeves gives the following most useful exercise, which must be 'diligently practised in order to unite the head-voice with the chest, and also to develop the head voice'. A note is chosen in the upper middle part of the singer's voice:

Attack the note firmly, but not loudly, using a closed vowel. Begin in the chest voice—swell the tone out to its fullest capacity without straining—let the tone die away imperceptibly. In this *diminuendo* the singer must be careful not to let the voice crack into *falsetto*, for then the whole purpose of the exercise is spoiled. When the chest tone has been diminished sufficiently, the voice will acquire a sort of veiled resonance, and the vibration at the root of the nose will be felt very distinctly. If the singer can make this veiled resonant tone swell without changing colour, or passing back into the chest tone, the secret of the head voice (or *mezza voce* as it is also called) has been acquired. Let it be reiterated that a crescendo on a *falsetto* note is impossible . . . In all exercises for the training of the head voice, the student must beware of nasal production.

In this exercise, the change from full voice to *mezza voce* must be accompanied by a strongly felt laryngeal OO, and a slight raising of the body's centre of gravity—the physical adjustment associated with a strong feeling of wonder or apprehension. (See the section 'Mood' in the chapter 'Colour'.)

At one time I took lessons from a very fine Italian baritone, trained in the old school. He taught almost entirely by example (he had perfect posture and, presumably because it was natural to him, he seemed to be unaware of its importance, and never mentioned the subject); virtually his only instructions were:

Qui largo (Here there must be space). [Pointing to the back of his neck.]
Qui piccolo (Here it must be small). [Pointing to the very top of his nose, between his eyes.]

In other words: Open up the resonating spaces, particularly the pharynx and oesophagus, and activate the voice, controlled from a point of concentration between the eyes.

The *imposto* is in practice dependent on, but not the same as, head resonance, nor is it the same as what is often called 'the focus of the voice'. It is not the centre of a reaction, but is a point of concentration from which the whole act of singing can most precisely be controlled. I find it helpful to think of it, not so much as the control centre for the voice, but as the control centre for singing.

This strong feeling for the head-voice and for vocal control from the *imposto* has led some writers to believe that the actual sound mechanism is in the head. Clearly this cannot be true—the sound is produced, by whatever means, in the larynx. The other view is that the sensations of which I write are 'merely' resonant reactions. I believe that this is also false. The *imposto*, as described, provides a control mechanism; its application accords with the experience of too many great singers to be so easily dismissed.

Many singers find it easier to localize this control centre if its purely physical aspect is first brought into play. An easy, but by no means the only, way of locating and activating the physical *imposto* is as follows (it helps at first to close the eyes, to help concentration):

1. With the nasal and pharyngeal spaces open, feel the clear distinction between the route taken by air through the nasal passages in normal breathing, and the higher—much higher—sniffing route. (I remember a soprano colleague once saying: 'If I can feel cold air going up into the middle of my head, I know that my

voice will be in order and that I will be able to sing well.')

2. Sniff, as though suddenly surprised by an unusual smell.
3. Close the sniffing route, as though protecting yourself from obnoxious fumes.

You will notice that as you make the closure at the root of the nose, which requires great concentration, the glottis closes in sympathy. Starting the note from this region will give a clean attack. (Note that the *imposto* is at the very top of the root of the nose—very close to, and energized from, the 'third eye'; if you try to perform this attack from too low a position it will sound unpleasantly nasal, and will not serve its purpose of fine control of the larynx.) You will quickly understand why, in the old Viennese school, this was called the *Hochgriff*—the high grip.

If this *imposto* grip is correctly activated, you will also observe an immediate reaction in the pelvic region. In fact you will be able to observe that the intention does more than just guide the impulse; it also actually swiches it on. In motoring terms, it provides a complete control panel.

Lamperti said:

It is a strange fact that the throat is controlled by what happens above it, in the acoustics of the head . . . And stranger still that the lungs are dominated by the muscular system below them, in waist, abdomen, and pelvis . . . Head and pelvis are mysteriously connected by coordination of all activities that lie between them.

This connection can only be activated from above—not from below. This is important; any attempt to find the *imposto* by pushing from below into a place where the singer imagines it to be, will result in unhealthy tension, and be totally counter-productive. Once the *imposto* is well established, its connection with the centre of balance and strength in the lower belly can be felt quite clearly.

At the risk of proving tedious to my readers, I must repeat: all this description is useless if applied in a purely physical way. Just as the impulse must arise from a genuine inner need to sing, so the intention must always come from the singer's

wish to make music, and to communicate—not in a generalized way, but with the utmost precision and concentration.
They must, like Maria Callas, 'know the score'; how otherwise
can the finely tuned mental and physical coordination which
good singing requires be activated?

Colour

One of the most important aspects of singing, and one which seems to be more and more neglected, is the ability consciously and meaningfully to vary the colour of the voice; to cultivate not only voice but also modifications of voice; in fact, to cultivate those aspects most directly expressive of human feelings, most characteristic of solo singing in our best tradition. Singers are frequently exhorted to vary the colour, but are too often at a loss to know precisely what is meant, and how to set about it. Too often they attempt to do this either through 'colouring' the voice superficially by distorting words, or resorting to states of excessive personal excitement.

Vocal colour is the result of bodily changes associated with changing emotions, feelings, and moods, which cause variations in the basic vocal sound. This vocal expressiveness is inseparably bound up with other forms of human expression. A person with inexpressive eyes, an inexpressive face, or an inflexible, inexpressive body, will normally have an inflexible and inexpressive voice, however sonorous or efficiently schooled it may be.

Then there are changes of colour coming from purely musical considerations. The human voice has a very special quality—namely the ability to vary the harmonic content of any note which is sung. A singer, confronted with a passage written in a major key, instinctively adapts his vocal mechanism and resonances so as to imply the appropriate tonality, whereas a passage in a minor key evokes, or should evoke, a very different response. An acute awareness of the harmony or the implied harmony of a particular phrase is essential to good singing and one of the most important weapons in the armoury of the singer-interpreter.

Lastly there are changes resulting from purely verbal elements, which, if correctly produced, should not interfere with the basic vocal colours. Exaggerated verbal colours should not be used as a substitute for genuine vocal colour.

These adjustments for differing colours—these modifications of voice—come about automatically, in response to the workings of the imagination; but this can only come about if the singer's technique permits. Conscious awareness of the different aspects of vocal modification, the extent of their autonomy, and the ability to differentiate between them in practice, is essential for vocal interpretation at the highest level.

The soundness of singers' vocal method can be judged from their ability to vary and modulate vocal sound in response to the musical, poetic, and dramatic contents of what is being sung. Flexibility in every regard is indeed one of the most important aspects of vocal technique. This does not mean simply the ability to sing quick passages of coloratura; it means that singers must be able to respond at will and with precision to the finest shades of the musical, poetic, and dramatic meaning.

In an important paper published in the *Journal of the Acoustical Society of America* in 1957, Professor D. B. Fry and Lucie Manén attempted to establish a basic system of classification for the main elements which give character to vocal performance. They wrote: 'Artistic performance by the singer depends largely on three factors: the singer's ability to characterize, i.e. to adopt a particular *voice quality*, the ability to portray an emotional *mood* and last, the ability to *articulate* a sequence of words while preserving continuity of musical tone.' In order to limit the scope of their investigation, they restricted the classifications to three in each of the categories I have mentioned above: three voice qualities, three moods, and three basic articulations. Their findings indicated that the changes in these three categories resulted in modifications in significantly different ranges of the harmonic spectrum. Of course, in practice, the variations are virtually infinite, but the principles involved I find extremely helpful. What their investigations confirmed was the extent of the possible conscious variations in vocal colour, and the extent to which these variations were the result of different adjustments, and therefore capable of a high degree of autonomy.

It is important to remember that what follows is a simplified version of infinitely variable characteristics.

Voice Qualities

First the three voice qualities: *light* voice, *lyric* voice, and *dramatic* voice. These three qualities are available to all singers, and are not simply a description of the size and weight of individual voices. Every singer should be able to use *their own* light, lyric, and dramatic qualities, and should be able to adopt these qualities at will, as may be appropriate to the character they are portraying, and the character of the music they are singing.

This is important for operatic characterization, and equally for the recitalist, who must be able to change character, and call upon as great a spectrum of vocal colours as possible during the course of a single recital. How often have I come away from a song recital with the impression that I have heard the same song sung twenty times, with no real variation of vocal timbre—all showing Mr X or Ms Y at their unvarying beautiful, most characteristic, and in the end boring, best!

These different voice qualities result mainly from a singer's use of different regions of resonance, and depend on differing degrees of emotional involvement and associated feelings of physical lightness or heaviness.

The appropriate physical adjustments required for the three basic qualities can be obtained by adopting the position for *voicing* 'b', 'd', and 'g' respectively.

Practical Hints

You may have observed that there are three types of yawning. There is the normal medium yawn which opens and stretches the back of the throat—the middle region of the pharynx. Then there is the high yawn which stretches the part of the pharynx behind and above the soft palate—the yawn that

makes your eyes water. Lastly there is the wonderful deep
yawn which seems to open up the whole body. By localizing
these three yawning regions (not actually yawning, but sensing the appropriate regions, rather like the *beginning* of a
yawn), and combining them with the voiced 'b', 'd', and 'g'
consonants, it is easy to make the necessary adjustments for
light, lyric, and dramatic voices. Emphasis is given to the
upper pharyngeal resonating space ('b' and high yawn), for
light voice. To this is *added* the medium pharyngeal space ('d'
and medium yawn) for lyric voice, and the lower space ('g'
and deep yawn) for dramatic voice. At the same time, resonators in progressively lower areas of the chest are caused to
react. It is important that the upper spaces are always used,
and the lower spaces progressively added. As I have already
said, this dividing into three sections is a great simplification,
because in practice these adjustments are not sudden changes
of gear, but continuously blend and combine with each
other.

These qualities are also associated with the feeling of balance in the body. Try walking lightly and quickly across the
room (Light), then walk 'normally' (Lyric), and finally walk
with a heavy portentous tread (Dramatic).

The voice qualities can be represented diagramatically as in
Table 1.

The use of the different qualities depends on the character
being portrayed, and is also dependent on the style of the
music being sung. The growth of the verismo style in Italian
and German opera, for example, leaned much more heavily
on intensely realistic dramatic involvement of the characters,

Table 1

Light	Lyric	Dramatic
Voiced b	Voiced d	Voiced g
High yawn	Medium yawn	Deep yawn
Light walk	Normal walk	Portentous walk

and therefore used the dramatic voice quality much more frequently than had been the case in earlier styles, where elegance of expression was expected to modify the extremes of emotional involvement.

It is important that casting directors should understand this particular modification of voice. Mistakes of casting are frequently made as a result of a failure of such understanding. Let me take an example of a role, originally written for a lyric soprano, which has recently often been assigned to a mezzo-soprano, or dramatic soprano, with significant, and I believe unfortunate, consequences.

The role of Der Komponist in Richard Strauss's opera *Ariadne auf Naxos* was always cast by Strauss as a lyric soprano. It requires the singer to use her dramatic quality for much of the opera. This is because the character, throughout, is in a state of extreme emotional involvement. Mezzo-sopranos, or heavy dramatic sopranos, normally find it necessary to *lighten* their voices, or to force the upper register, in order to sing the music assigned to this character. Now the superficial sound of a natural lyrical soprano singing with her full dramatic quality, and a mezzo-soprano or dramatic soprano singing with her lighter lyrical quality is very similar; but the effect on the public is profoundly different. As Charles Darwin wrote: 'The effect [of a song] is seen to depend not merely on the actual sounds, but also in part on the nature of the action which produces the sounds.' Any intensity which the public feels when a mezzo-soprano sings this role will tend to reflect the singer's struggle to sing phrases which lie uncomfortably high for her voice (a source of embarrassed discomfort, or at best a feeling of strained hysteria) rather than the intensity produced by the deep dramatic commitment of the young composer. Anyone who heard Irmgard Seefried, Sena Jurinac, or Elizabeth Söderström, all sopranos, in this role, will know exactly what I mean.

Singers are not equally adept at using all the voice qualities. Casting and choice of repertoire do depend to a large extent on individual vocal characteristics. But every dramatic soprano—even the heaviest—should be able to use *her* light voice (which of course does not suddenly turn her into a soubrette) and every soubrette should be capable of using *her* dramatic voice (which again does not turn her into Brünnhilde), for the purposes of characterization. In the case of sopranos, for example, it should be, and in the past was, considered quite normal, for one soprano to adjust her voice to be able to sing all the three female parts in Offenbach's *Tales of Hoffmann*, as did Lilli Lehmann. In more recent times, Elizabeth Söderström has sung all three soprano roles in *Der Rosenkavalier* (within the same season).

Formerly this would be considered quite normal; today this ability to vary the voice quality is a rarity, and is even considered somehow suspect! Recently a young pupil of mine suggested to the management of her German opera-house that she would like to sing all three Offenbach roles—which she could easily have done. The response was: 'You must decide what sort of voice category you belong to. You will never get on in this profession unless you stick to one thing.' Is it not sad, when a high degree of artistic and professional skill is actually frowned upon by those who are entrusted with the management and direction of our opera-houses?

There is one thing to be borne in mind. These voice qualities are variations within the natural limitations of each individual singer. It would of course be nonsense to suppose that a naturally light-voiced soprano should be able to sing Isolde. Natural weight or robustness of voice is not the same thing as the dramatic quality that I have described. A naturally heavy voice will still be heavier than a naturally light voice, even when using its light quality.

All this was clearly understood, for example, by Gounod, who in his opera *Roméo et Juliette* requires a great range of voice quality for his Juliette. She starts the opera as a very innocent young girl; her opening aria (the famous waltz song) requires the soprano to use her *light* voice quality in a typical coloratura aria. As she matures through her experience of love to the final tragic end, her music graduates through *lyric* quality to *dramatic* quality in her final aria. For this reason, the final aria is more often than not omitted, as being 'too

heavy' for the soprano cast as Juliette. In fact the role needs
a much more robust voice than is often supposed by those
who imagine the first aria to be typical of the whole role.
Juliette should be sung by a soprano able to use all three voice
qualities. (Gounod himself appears to have been an accomplished singer, and in his music frequently shows a high level
of understanding of vocal possibilities.)

Verdi made the very similar demands upon his Gilda. Her
music shows her personal, and hence vocal, development—
something which is all too seldom heard in the opera-
house.

The role of Dr Malatesta in Donizetti's opera *Don
Pasquale* is a distinctly frivolous character. The general style
of the music, with its rather heavy orchestration, demands
that it should be sung by a lyric baritone with real 'operatic'
robustness. But it must be sung with that singer's light-lyric
quality if the elegance and gaiety of the character is to be
realized. The same singer, if he is to sing the role of, say,
Valentin in Gounod's *Faust*, must use his dramatic quality.
Valentin is young, so the role is written for a basically lyrical
singer. But he is extremely passionate, and therefore must use
his full dramatic quality.

I well remember hearing the great Norwegian soprano
Ingrid Bjoner singing a beautifully poised, youthful sounding
Desdemona in Verdi's *Otello*, a few days after she had been
singing Ortrud in Wagner's *Lohengrin*—probably the heaviest role ever written for a dramatic soprano—usually assigned
to a very robust mezzo-soprano. I congratulated her after the
performance, and she said: 'I was taught to develop my head
voice, and to let it always lead, and I learned how to use my
lighter quality. I can always come back to them, because they
are always there.'

One grave disadvantage of the contemporary system of
casting operas is that singers are to a greater and greater
extent type-cast, so that they do not in general have the
opportunity of cultivating the ability to make these particular
adjustments to anything like the extent that they did in the
past, when singers, as ensemble members, were expected to

perform a far greater variety of roles. It is sad for the professional singers of today, that with this increasing tendency to
type-cast operas, they are often denied the sheer pleasure of
playing the chameleon, and singing a wide and varied repertoire, demanding the use of all their different voice qualities;
denied the possibility of discovering their full expressive
range and imaginative powers.

Mood

The whole body reacts to different moods by adjustments of
posture and of the larynx. These adjustments affect the colour
of the voice and on the primitive level are expressed by
emotional exclamations, which have the character of different primitive vowel-sounds. These variations are quite separate from those associated with the different qualities that I
have described above, and which are concerned primarily
with different resonances.

As was explained to me by Professor Denis Fry, a pioneer
in the science of phonetics, it is important for singers to be
able to distinguish between the exclamatory vowels, produced at the level of the larynx with the involvement of the
whole body, and the vowels of articulation, formed in the
mouth as in normal speech. The former not only express, but
also arouse, quite distinct feelings, and are controlled by the
primitive, instinctive part of the brain. The latter are produced by the lips, tongue, and palate, and are controlled by
the most recently developed part of the brain—that concerned with speech. These two vowel-producing mechanisms
are combined during singing, but can be, and as far as possible should be, emancipated from each other. The exclamatory vowels—the vowels of phonation—are associated
with strongly felt moods, are universal, and, as Fry explained
to me, can often be observed, for example 'in emotional
exclamations of children before they have fully acquired
articulate speech, or by adults in whom diseases of the
cortex eliminate the coordination needed for the highest
levels of speech integration'. Unless these exclamatory vowels

are produced with the involvement of the whole body, the result will lack conviction, and will cause unhealthy vocal tension.

Of course, the variations of mood are, in practice, virtually infinite; there are, however, three primary moods, rather like the three primary colours, which I think can usefully be considered, if only as a help towards awareness of the possible range of those variations. These primary moods are expressed as vocal exclamations:

1. The mood of aggression or distaste, or sheer determination. Its most primitive vocal expression is the exclamation EE!
2. The mood of joy or contentment. Expressed as AA!
3. The mood of fear , apprehension or wonder. Expressed as OO!

These basic moods, can be represented diagramatically as shown in Table 2.

The mood (and vowel-sound) appropriate to any vocal music can be placed somewhere along the line between EE , through AA, to OO.

Table 2

Aggression	Contentment	Fear
Attack	Repose	Retreat
EE	AA	OO

PRACTICAL HINTS

Try to feel these basic moods, and observe how the body, including the vocal organs, reacts. You can then reproduce these adjustments as appropriate for any song you choose to sing. It is essential that these moods come from genuine feelings, involving the whole body, and are not merely conceptualized imitations.

Such adjustments can only be practised by really giving oneself over to the imagination; by imagining scenes which evoke different mood responses. Once established, they can be reproduced at will.

Stand with a good, well-balanced posture, the whole body alert, open, and ready to react. Imagine a scene where in this alert state you are surprised by some occurrence which causes a reaction of apprehension, expressed by the exclamation OO! Observe your reactions as you prepare to withdraw in fear. (The OO must be sung without help from the lips.)

Now imagine a variation of this scene which causes you to react with aggression. This is expressed by the exclamation EE! Observe your reactions as you prepare to attack.

Lastly imagine yourself surprised by an occurrence which causes a feeling of great joy. The exclamation is AA!, and you are happy to remain where you are, in a state of great (active) contentment. Again, observe your reactions.

These exclamatory vowels are one of the main elements in determining vocal colour. They are independent of speech, of language, and of the voice quality being used.

If you doubt this, continue the above excercise as follows: Establish a happy AA mood, and sing a long note in this colour. Then, *without changing the* basic mood, articulate the five vowel-sounds: i, e, a, o, u.

Now do the same with the basic OO mood and then the EE mood. You will find that it is possible to articulate all the vowel-sounds clearly, *without so-called vowel modification*, in all of the vocal mood-colours.

Next sing the above exercises in light voice quality, lyric quality, and dramatic quality.

One of the greatest faults to be heard among singers is caused by a lack of understanding of the distinction between exclamatory vowels of phonation and vowels of articulation. Failure to distinguish between these two forms of vocal modification can often result in changes of basic vocal colour being made with every new spoken vowel, or, in an attempt to avoid this, distortion of the vowels of articulation. How often have we heard tenors singing in Handel's *Messiah*, 'Comfort ye my people'; a warm, comforting tone on the word 'Comfort' followed by pure aggression on 'ye' and 'p-eo-ple'. Sometimes, aware of the inappropriateness of the colour of their voices, they decide to 'modify' the vowel-sound, and sing something very like 'Comfort yer my purple', or even 'Cermvertyermerburble', in a vain attempt to produce a legato phrase by slurring all the consonants (also quite unnecessary, and indeed counter-productive). Recently, in the course of a major singing competition, I heard, 'Pace mio Dio' sung as 'Percermierderyer'—and the young soprano was awarded a prize!

This nonsense is simply the result of using vowels of phonation for purposes of articulation. It may be good practice for ventriloquists, but not for singers. It is another aspect of sloppy, imprecise diction which is dealt with in detail in the chapter 'The Importance of Good Diction', below. Clear, high-placed, forward diction together with continuity of vocal mood make modification of vowels of articulation quite unnecessary. It requires habits of speech very different from the slurred enunciation so often heard from singers, or the various forms of shouting cultivated by some actors.

There is one other aspect of this ability to respond to different moods which must be mentioned. It is a fact that the EE mood has the most limited vocal range. You cannot take this mood to the top of your voice without strain and loss of quality. The OO mood on the other hand, if properly produced, permits the voice to extend upwards with greater ease, and facilitates the use of the so-called head-voice, formerly synonymous with *mezza voce*. This of course means literally 'half-voice', but is correctly used to indicate a particular vocal colour, not simply quiet singing. It implies in fact singing with a strong OO mood, something which according to reports was the Caruso's way of dealing with what is known as the *passaggio*, or the transition to the top of the voice.

Frequently, singers who find difficulty in extending their range upwards, are hindered by their own determination. Determination tends to express itself in aggressive vocal adjustment (EE), which makes the upward extension impossible. Cultivating and practising feelings of wonder (OO) can usually do much to facilitate the development of the high range.

This classification of moods may appear to be a gross oversimplification. But a moment's thought will make it possible to place any mood somewhere along the line that I have described.

The most important thing to realize is that the vocal colour associated with mood should be produced by an adjustment of the whole body, not simply by the muscles of the larynx, nor by the parts (the lips, the front of the tongue) which are required for articulation.

The physical effects of awe or wonder are very like those produced by fear or apprehension. The reaction to seeing a beautiful sunset or a masterpiece of art is clearly well towards the 'OO' end of the spectrum, as are feelings of spiritual love. Excited sexual passion on the other hand contains a great deal of 'aggression', and moves at least part-way towards 'EE'.

The mood of a song is of course determined by the imagination, and if a singer is able to react with accuracy to the stimulus provided by the imagination, these changes will happen automatically. However, if singers have been trained only to produce one basic sound—the personal timbre corresponding to their own psychological make-up—as is so often the case, they are unable to react with the appropriate physical changes. It is therefore important for singers to be aware of the changes that occur with changing moods, and to be able to reproduce them at will. It is not then necessary, or even desirable, for them to feel the mood with full personal involvement every time a song is sung. But it is absolutely essential to have done so at some time, and to have observed the body's reactions.

There is a profound difference between changes of vocal colour which come from within, in the way I have described, and vocal 'colouring' which is imposed on a basic personal vocal sound. This superficial 'colouring' of the voice usually involves distorted diction, and frequently vocal strain. Although the 'real thing' may seem much more subtle, the actual effect on an audience is infinitely greater.

Let us now look at some examples:

Pure OO moods, and pure EE moods, being at the extreme ends of the spectrum, are of course the rarest. One of the clearest examples of the OO mood in the operatic repertoire is to be found in the tenor aria 'Una furtiva lagrima' from Donizetti's opera *L'elisir d'amore*. Here the singer is in a mood of great sadness, with feelings of rejection. For a moment he imagines that his girl loves him, and he changes briefly into the AA mood, only to return to OO as his doubts and fears return. There is a marvellous illustration of these mood-changes in an early recording by Enrico Caruso.

Examples of pure OO mood for the soprano appear in Pamina's aria 'Ach ich fühl's', and in the role of the Countess in Mozart's *Figaro*. The first aria 'Porgi amor' has pure OO mood throughout. The third-act aria begins with a strong OO as she regrets her past happiness (see Ex. 1*a*). But in the second part of the aria, when she hopes that perhaps the happy days may return, she moves distinctly towards AA (see Ex. 1*b*).

Ex. 1. Mozart, 'Dove sono', from *Le nozze di Figaro*, Act 3

(*a*) Contessa

(*b*) Contessa

Ex. 2. Wagner, 'O du mein holder Abendstern', from *Tannhäuser*, Act 3

For the baritone, one of the most obvious examples of the OO mood is the 'Abendstern' aria in Wagner's *Tannhäuser*. The mixture of wonder at the beauty of the night sky, spiritual love, and personal sadness give the aria a threefold reason for this mood. If sung with the true feelings appropriate to the mood, it can be an intensely moving aria. Sung, as it so often is, with a smooth, rather bland 'instrumental' sound, with no strong physical mood, it can seem to be boring and rather banal (see Ex. 2).

The danger of singing with such a strong OO mood, with its predominance of low harmonics, is that, unless the singer consciously adds high harmonics to the sound, he will tend to sound flat in pitch to the listener. (See the chapter 'The Pitch-Intensity Effect', below.)

This mood produces timbres which are very affecting, and indeed these timbres are often required by the vocal repertoire; so much so that I have heard singing defined as 'weeping to music'. For this reason some singers rely almost exclusively on this adjustment; some teachers encourage this. In particular, the older school of German teachers often insisted on this OO position as the essential prerequisite for good singing. The results can be very beautiful, but limited, if used exclusively. Such singers, faced by the wish to express other moods and feelings, tend to resort to non-vocal means of expression—exaggerated tricks of verbal 'colouring' and articulation, or excessive gesturing—in an attempt to convey subtleties of feeling which they are unable to convey by purely vocal means.

Although it is important for classical singing, this OO mood seems to be the most difficult for modern singers to acquire. Associated as it is with natural expression of feelings of wonder, of awe, of reverence, this could perhaps be a reflection on the lack of the strong experience of such feelings in modern life.

It is most important for singers to be able to distinguish between genuine changes of mood and character—of vocal colour—and mere changes of dynamics accompanied by verbal colouring.

It has unfortunately become something of a rarity for singers to be able to produce the wide range of vocal timbres associated with the best singing traditions. The most distinguishing feature of the genuine vocal moods is the extent to which listeners are touched, and are made to share in the mood being expressed by the singer, rather than simply hearing, and perhaps admiring from outside. The prevalence of studio recording, without audience, and with concentration on the more superficial aspects of vocal sound, has I believe played a large part in the neglect of this vital aspect of the interpretation of vocal music.

The most commonly used mood is of course AA, that of joy and contentment. It is the essential mood associated with so-called 'effortless singing'. It is the mood most practised in singing studios and produces the timbre most frequently cultivated. Superficially it is closest to the sound of singing without impulse and without intention. It is a useful general-purpose timbre, and can allow for a certain variation in tone-colour. But its exclusive cultivation by singers unaware of the range of timbres available to them is responsible for a great deal of bland singing, which seems to be all too easily accepted by critics and conductors, and even encouraged by recording producers.

The aggressive EE mood can be very exciting and exhilarating, but should be used by singers with great discretion. It is all too easy for singers wishing to express this mood to slip over into pressurizing and forcing their voices. They should also be aware that it is dangerous to try to use this mood when singing in the higher range. For sopranos, and naturally high sopranos in particular, it is all too easy to confuse the rich harmonics of the true head-voice with the shrill harmonics of the aggressive mood.

It is in the operatic repertoire where the pure aggressive mood is most often appropriate. Rigoletto has two outburst of naked aggression: first in the aria 'Cortigiani vil razza dannata'. (See Ex. 3*a*.) This outburst is immediately followed by a passage where Rigoletto, realizing that pure aggression is getting nowhere, turns to the other end of the mood-spectrum, with a passage where he tries to appeal to the better feelings of his tormentors. (See Ex. 3*b*.)

This big change from EE mood to OO mood, coupled with imaginative diction, can have a most profound effect, which the all-too-frequently heard AA mood throughout, with slight modifications, and changes of dynamics coupled with bursts of shouting, cannot have, because the primitive responses of, on the one hand, pure aggression, and on the other hand, awesome humility, have not been touched. The audience hear with their ears, but not with their hearts.

The second place for Rigoletto to show his aggression is in the 'vendetta' passage at the end of Act 3. (See Ex. 3*c*.)

It is largely because of the difficulty of performing these two passages with the appropriate colour that the role of Rigoletto has in modern times been assigned more and more frequently to singers with very heavy, robust voices, for whom the expression of aggression comes most easily—forgetting that a large part of the role is in fact written very lyrically. The tragic, intelligent, loving, paternal side of Rigoletto's character, as a result, is frequently missing in a performance, because the role has been cast with only these two moments of aggression in mind. It is important that the robust-voiced Rigoletto should also be able to use his lyrical quality, and a genuine *mezza voce*.

I have already quoted Charles Darwin. The whole passage from which I have quoted a short extract reads:

In songs . . . which express great vehemence of passion, the effect often chiefly depends on the forcible utterance of some one or two characteristic passages which demand great exertion of vocal force; and it will be frequently noticed that a song of this character fails in its proper effect

Ex. 3. Verdi, *Rigoletto*, showing changes in Rigoletto's mood in Act 3

(*a*) Rigoletto

(*b*) Rigoletto

(*c*) Rigoletto

when sung by a voice of sufficient power and range to give the characteristic passages without much exertion. This is, no doubt, the secret of
the loss of effect so often produced by the transposition of a song from
one key to another. The effect is thus seen to depend not merely on the
actual sounds, but also in part on the nature of the action which
produces the sounds. Indeed it is obvious that whenever we [the audi-
ence] feel the expression of a song . . . we are, in fact, interpreting the
muscular actions which produce sound.

Indeed, the ability to express vehemence of passion with
energy but without forcing the voice is one of the most
difficult skills for a singer to acquire.

As I have already said, the examples I have given are of rare
moments when extremes of mood are called for. Singers'
response to mood is governed by intuition, and if the body
and the whole vocal apparatus is in perfect balance, the
response will be automatic. They must, however, be aware of
the physical effects of differing moods; aware of the wide
range of variations of colour available to them, so that they
can reproduce them for artistic purposes without having con-
tinual recourse to states of personal excitement. They must in
fact be able to produce different moods by adjusting their
balance but without losing their poise.

Text

The third element which affects vocal colour is the text. I have
already stressed the importance, for singers, of being able to
distinguish between vowels of phonation, which are expressions of mood, and vowels of articulation, which are concerned with language and thought, are formed in the mouth,
and which have their own life, guided from the left brain. It
is vitally important that singers should be able to form clear
words, and be able to relish those words, without changing
the basic vocal colour or mood, unless of course such changes
are called for by the specific demands of the song.

The modifications of colour resulting from articulation are,
compared to those resulting from mood, a matter of surface
texture. The consonants must be clear, the vowel-sounds
pure. The feelings associated with those words are expressed

by the main body of the vocal sound which I have described in detail. These two elements should not be confused. The only way I know of avoiding this confusion is continually to be aware of its possibility. Diction and vocalization—word and tone—must always go hand in hand; they should not be separated, but must be differentiated and as far as possible emancipated from each other. A singer must be able to enunciate clearly both vowels and consonants without disturbing the underlying vocal colour (mood), and must be able to change the mood without distorting the purity of the diction. It is the words, together with the musical form, that convey the composer's thoughts. The vocal tone communicates the feelings associated with those thoughts. The art of interpretation demands the utmost clarity and precision of both these aspects. Muddled generalization is always the enemy of art.

Harmony

The last element affecting vocal colour is harmony. The human voice, unlike most 'melodic' instruments, can vary its harmonics so as to be able to imply harmony as well as pitch. Indeed it is very advantageous for singers to think of themselves as an harmonic rather than as a purely melodic instrument. If a singer is aware that his voice vibrates with a whole spectrum of harmonics, which are almost infinitely variable, he will realize that he can sing a single note, not only in a wide range of timbres, but also with varying purely harmonic musical content. It should be possible, for example to sing a G in the middle of the voice

1. as the tonic of G Major
2. as the tonic of G Minor
3. as the fifth of C Major
4. as the fifth of C Minor, and so on.

These differences should be clearly audible, and should be simply the result of allowing the voice to be led by the musical imagination, the inner ear.

Gerald Moore, in his reminiscences, tells how Elena Gerhardt was able to do this. He writes as though this ability were a rare feat. It should be an essential skill of every singer. It is not in the least difficult. It simply requires that singers should have a clear awareness of the harmonic content and implication of any phrase that they sing, and a singing technique sufficiently flexible to be able to respond.

There is one final and most important thing to say about modifications of colour. The basic qualities and moods, together with the harmony, the broad underlying colours of the voice are associated with bodily attitude; in particular, posture and balance. The subtleties of expression—the surface details—are closer to the feeling for the colours of words, and to the expression in the face and the eyes. An inexpressive face and inexpressive eyes result in singing lacking subtlety and refinement of expression. How many singers, or would-be singers, have I met whose faces and whose eyes are full of vitality and expression while in normal conversation, but who lose all that vitality the moment they start to vocalize. I use the word 'vocalize', because I cannot describe their activity as singing. It is what I call the 'dead codfish syndrome'. Just as the region of the eyes is the centre of expressiveness and communication in normal daily intercourse, so it should be the centre of expressiveness when singing.

In view of all this, I suggest that singers should make a conscious decision as to the intended quality and mood *every time they sing*. This applies not only to the preparation of vocal music, but also to vocal exercises. As the Irish singing teacher Molloy said, in Robertson Davies's novel *A Mixture of Frailties*:

The muhd's [mood] everything. Get it, and you'll get the rest. If you don't get it, all the *fiorituri* and exercises in agility and *Legato* in the world'll be powerless to make a good singer of you. The muhd's at the root of all. And that's what I teach my beginners, and my advanced pupils, and some who've gone out into the world and made big names, but who come back now and again for a brush-up or some help with special problems. And mostly it all boils down to the muhd.

Singers should have all aspects of colour at their disposal. It is perfectly possible to sing with well-developed voice quality and mood, but without any of the 'surface detail', associated with the text, which gives clarity to the content, and subtlety to the expression. Such deficient singers are generally thought of as 'typical opera-singers'. On the other hand, there are singers who cultivate only subtlety of surface detail, without ever developing the more 'primitive' aspects—quality and mood. Such singers, lacking the direct appeal which comes from the communication of character, emotions, and feelings, are thought of as 'typical recitalists'.

However accomplished, they are both in reality only half-singers. Complete singers, whatever the personal characteristics of voice and temperament which lead them to a particular choice of repertoire, should, within the natural limits of their physique and temperament, have all these things at their disposal.

Falsetto

All the modifications of voice that I have described can be blended into each other in response to subtle variations of character, mood, and harmony, as required by the singer's imagination. This blending—starting and finishing with *mezza voce*, and developing on the way into a full voice—is known as *messa di voce* (putting forth the voice), and has in the past always been considered to be an essential skill for all singers. (See the section 'Practical Hints' in the chapter 'Impulse, Intention, and the Anacrusis', above.)

There is one vocal colour which cannot be blended smoothly into this varying spectrum; that is the false voice, or falsetto, which stands apart as a separate, and special, colour. For this reason, it has been banned by many writers on the subject of solo singing from Caccini onwards, until recent times, when it has been widely cultivated.

Caccini, the founding father of post-Renaissance solo singing, specifically forbids the use of the falsetto voice as being unsuitable for the natural expression of emotion that his 'new music' demands. In the preface to *Le nuove musiche* he writes:

Let [the singer] choose a key in which he can sing in a full, natural voice, avoiding falsetto. . . . From the falsetto voice no nobility of good singing can arise; that comes from a natural voice, comfortable throughout the whole range, able to be controlled at will, [and] with the breath used only to demonstrate mastery of all the affects necessary for this most noble manner of singing.

The male falsetto voice, however beautiful, produces vocal sound with minimal *direct* emotional content; that is its particular character, and indeed, in the right context, its strength. The falsetto voice cannot be developed from the direct emotional exclamations of which I have written, so that the 'modifications of voice' resulting from this direct connection are not possible. For this reason, historically it has been used in European music, apart from in certain folk traditions, almost exclusively as a voice for choral singing; in particular in Church music, where its ethereal, impersonal, unearthly, instrumental, quality is especially appropriate, and can be very beautiful and effective, precisely because of this lack of direct emotional content. In the main stream of solo singing though, its use has been, until recently, almost exclusively for 'special' effects—often comic.

As so frequently in the world of singing, there has been much confusion over terminology. Some writers have even used the word 'falsetto' to indicate what is more generally known as 'mixed voice'. Some modern writers have confused 'falsetto' and 'head-voice', and modern falsettists frequently misuse that term to describe their vocal activity. The two are totally different; instructions for developing the head-voice almost invariably warn quite specifically against slipping over into falsetto, for indeed it is virtually impossible to develop the true head-voice from a falsetto attack.

In Italy, it was at one time the practice to castrate boys before puberty, in order to preserve the high pitch of their voices. I suggest that one possible reason for the growth of this practice was to enable men to sing at a high pitch *without resorting to the use of falsetto*; to be able to sing brilliantly and strongly at this high pitch while preserving the direct emotional content.

The castrato voice was, vocally speaking, a *natural* voice, capable of all the modifications needed for expressive singing, in particular the *messa di voce*. It is interesting at a time like the present, when so much is spoken about 'authenticity', that these distinctions should be so widely ignored. The developments of the Renaissance, which led to the music of Monteverdi, for example, demanded that solo singing should become a means of giving the direct natural dimension of feeling to the declaimed words. Apart from his declared aims, the actual range of Monteverdi's vocal music—restricted to that range where such expressiveness is most easily achieved—only serves to confirm this. The use, in this music, of the falsetto voice, incapable by its very nature of the type of direct expressiveness which is the very essence of the dramatic music of Monteverdi and his contemporaries and followers, cannot, I suggest, be considered truly authentic (unless pitch is considered the only criterion).

Falsetto singing can be very beautiful, when appropriate, as used traditionally, for example, in certain choral- and folk-traditions, in Alpine mountain yodelling, or, particularly in England, where the practice of castration for artistic purposes never took on, primarily in Church music. It is because of this special, ethereal, quality that Benjamin Britten used this voice for the role of Oberon in *A Midsummer Night's Dream*, and again for the role of Apollo—contrasting with Dionysus—in *Death in Venice*. However, the falsetto voice is no proper substitute either for the 'natural' high castrato voice or the 'natural' unbroken boy's voice. Its characteristics are different and special, but in the main stream of the European classical tradition of which I write, it must be considered as a 'special effect'.

The Importance of Good Diction

Musick and poetry, have ever been acknowledged Sisters, which walking hand in hand, support each other: As poetry is the harmony of words, so musick is that of notes: and as poetry is a rise above prose and oratory, so is Musick the exaltation of poetry. Both of them may excell apart, but sure they are most excellent when they are joind; because nothing is then wanting to either of their perfections: for thus they appear like wit & beauty in the same person. (Dryden)

A Master that disregards Recitative, probably does not understand Words, and then how can he ever instruct a Scholar in Expression, which is the Soul of vocal Performance, and without which it is impossible to sing well? (Tosi)

It is not only beauty of voice which distinguishes with singularity the virtuoso, but also the excellent method of reciting which he should be able to produce, and which will win approbation and great reward. (Mancini)

Writing of his lessons in Milan in the middle of the last century with Gaetano Nava, Sir Charles Santley says: 'He insisted that the object of music was to give greater expression and emphasis to the words, and for this reason never allowed a syllable to be neglected. "I must hear what you are singing about," he would say, "or I cannot tell how you are singing, and, consequently, cannot help you!"'

Vocal sound must, in every way, be *appropriate* to the thoughts and sentiments expressed by the words. Those words need to be heard clearly.

Sims Reeves wrote: 'Pronunciation and eloquence are synonymous terms to the singer. Good Pronunciation at once enlists the sympathies of an audience.'

Enrico Caruso wrote: 'Certainly no singer can be called a great artist unless his diction is good, for a beautiful voice alone will not make up for other deficiencies. A singer endowed with a small voice, or even one of not very pleasing quality, can often give more pleasure than a singer posessing a big impressive voice, but no diction.'

We live at a time when diction is sadly neglected by singers in general. We are frequently told that it is impossible to hear the text in an opera-house, or large concert hall, particularly when singers have big or beautiful voices, or are singing a legato line. Those who propagate such nonsense clearly never heard the many singers from an earlier generation who loved and relished the sound and meaning of words, and who considered clear declamation to be an essential part of good singing; quite apart from some notable singers still performing, who are capable of combining a legato singing line with clear, imaginative diction. Anyone listening, though, to recordings of singers made over the whole period of recording cannot but observe the steady decline in the standard of diction, and of declamation; and this in spite of the enormous improvement in recording techniques

This decline has, I believe, gone hand in hand with the decrease in the number of vernacular performances. When audiences expect to hear and to understand what singers are singing about, then those singers are encouraged to express themselves through words as well as through vocal sounds. If the singers are performing in a language that they themselves understand only poorly, and which the audience in general understands not at all, then quite simply they do not bother with the diction. But in the process they rob themselves and their audience of one of the chief means of dramatic and poetic expression—one of their chief means of communication. Members of the audience either spend too much energy in wondering what it is all about, or, uncomprehending, just allow the sounds to wash over them. The performance becomes generalized, and ultimately mediocre.

This is not to suggest that all performances should be in the vernacular; but I do suggest most strongly that good habits of diction, declamation, and communication are most easily acquired by young singers through use of their mother-tongue, and singing to audiences who can understand.

As a jury member of many international singing competitions, I have often observed how comparatively uninteresting singers come to life when they sing something in their own language.

There is a widespread misunderstanding among singers about the matter of diction. They seem to believe—are even often encouraged to believe—that clear diction interferes with the flow of vocal sound, and they therefore cultivate a lazy form of enunciation. In fact the very opposite is the case.

Professor D. B. Fry and Lucie Manén write:

> The singer has to superimpose upon the activity of phonation the articulation required by the language he is using. This he does by cortical control of those parts of the mechanism not required in phonation—the forepart of the tongue, the palate, and the lips. One of the difficulties which face the singer is that of producing the required articulations without interfering with the appropriate voice quality and mood provided by the phonation.

The first, and most important step towards overcoming these 'difficulties' is, I suggest, quite simply to be aware of the difference between vowels of phonation and vowels of articulation. (See the section 'Mood' in the chapter 'Colour', above.)

Singers using a lazy, 'relaxed', imprecise, diction usually attempt to use vowels of phonation for the purposes of speech, thereby interfering with the vocal timbres; the vowels of articulation should be formed in the mouth, not in the larynx, and should not interfere with voice production. Consonants should be formed clearly and precisely with the forward part of the tongue, and with the lips. Lazy, imprecise consonants use the back part of the tongue, and throw the words on to the parts needed for vocalization. Clear, crisp, forward articulation of the text can to a large extent emancipate the parts required for diction, and leave those needed for vocalization uncluttered. The practice of clear diction, in fact, helps to concentrate and free the voice. As Enrico Caruso wrote: 'I would aver that a fine enunciation, far from interfering with it, aids voice production, makes it softer and more concentrated.'

Many singers, unaware of the distinction between vowels

of phonation and of articulation, and unable to use differing *vocal* moods, try to imitate characteristics of these moods by artificial 'colouring' of the vowels of articulation. This so-called 'vowel-modification' is not only unnecessary, it can be extremely distasteful to any listener of discernment. This practice also completely destroys the direct instinctive contact of feeling and mood between singer and audience.

I learned an old way of practising good emancipated articulation from a friend of the great baritone Friedrich Schorr (a model of perfect legato singing, combined with clear and imaginative diction), for whom it was a daily exercise. This, the best way that I have found of training the lips and the foward part of the tongue to articulate clearly, is to practise silently; to articulate the words without voice—not even whispering—being sure the while to maintain an open throat, and an internal smile. This practice is also strongly recommended by Olga Averino. In this way the singer becomes progressively more aware of the small, precise, energetic movements necessary for good articulation, and can avoid on the one hand, slovenly habits of diction, and on the other hand the equally bad habit of 'mouthing the words', involving excessive movements of the jaw, both of which interfere with smooth vocalization.

A helpful exercise is as follows:

With a well-established alert and buoyant posture, and open throat (the inner smile helps here, as always),

1. Sing a short sentence at a convenient pitch in the middle of the voice. For this the jaw should, as always, be opened as for chewing, approximately one thumb's width.
2. Without allowing the instrument to 'collapse', or the jaw to change its adjustment, whisper the same sentence.
3. Again, maintaining the buoyancy and readiness to sing, speak the sentence silently, without any movement of breath, and without exaggerated jaw movements.

In this way it is possible to become progressively more aware of the small precise movements of the lips and the front part of the tongue, appropriate to precise diction.

Another help towards achieving clarity of diction, and enabling the consonants to assist in concentrating and focusing the voice is to remember that the consonants, particularly those at the beginning of a word, should always come a fraction before the sung vowel, so that the vowel-sound comes on the beat musically; and also that, in the case of sounding consonants, they should have the same pitch as the following vowel. Even non-sounding consonants should *mentally* be pronounced at the pitch of the following sung vowel-sound. The time taken by consonants, which, apart from special effects, should be as short as possible, should always be taken from the preceding vowel-sound. This is particularly important in slow-moving legato singing.

Johannes Messchaert gives the example shown in Ex. 4.

Despite the often-repeated claim that singers of the so-called 'Bel Canto' school of singing were solely interested in beautiful sound, I can find no evidence for this. Indeed, every writer on singing from this period that I have seen insists on the importance of clear crisp diction as an essential element in any vocal performance. The quotations at the beginning of this chapter are typical examples. I have the impression that the neglect of diction is almost entirely a phenomenon of the second half of the twentieth century.

It is often stated that the Italian language is particularly suitable for good singing. This is unquestionably so; indeed, European classical singing has, to a large extent, grown out of

Ex. 4. Johannes Messchaert, *Eine Gesangsstunde*, illustration of the timing of consonants, using an example from Schubert, 'Meeres Stille', D216

the Italian language. The pure, open vowel sounds of Italian are usually given the credit. What is often forgotten is the importance of Italian consonants, which are exceptionally crisp, and which are not explosive—rather the opposite. The Italian 'p' for example is produced by a vigorous separation of the lips, *not* by forcing air through the closed lips in the English or German fashion. The cultivation of Italian consonants is of the utmost benefit to singers vocally, quite apart from the benefit to clear diction. Indeed, 'special' habits of diction cultivated by English, French, and German singers have always tended to the use of Italianate consonant production, especially when, as in German, some consonants are produced gutturally in normal everyday speech.

Good, old-fashioned advice is given by Sir Charles Santley, who, like Friedrich Schorr, was renowned for the excellence of his diction combined with perfect legato:

The consonants must be pronounced promptly and firmly, using the tongue, the teeth, and the lips—otherwise the words will not be distinct and their sense will be lost. . . . The mouth ought not to open more than sufficient to introduce the tip of a finger; if the lower jaw is lowered beyond what is necessary for this it is impossible to pronounce the consonants promptly and firmly, as the tongue, teeth and lips will be too far apart to fulfil their office. Moreover, the wagging of the lower jaw is destructive of any expression of sentiment the countenance ought to display.

The most advantageous, and at the same time the most pleasing and elegant position of the mouth is the approach to a smile, all the muscles of the face being kept perfectly supple so as to be ready to second every change of expression occurring in the work the performer is engaged on, but without exaggeration; there is but one step from the sublime to the ridiculous, which exaggeration would inevitably make.

Clear diction is associated with clear thought. Without clear thought, our goal of good interpretation is impossible. If we are to avoid the all-too-frequent habit of merely making agreeable, generalized vocal noises, on to which words are (often reluctantly) superimposed, then all singing should begin with a clear idea, a clear feeling, a clearly established mood. Clear diction comes, not as a result of mouthing or spitting out the words, but first and foremost as a result of putting the words into the forefront of the mind, and then of cultivating the maximum possible emancipation of the muscles involved in articulation from those needed for vocalization; thus helping to free the voice to express the feelings associated with the words. This precision of diction requires regular and diligent exercise, which can be carried out silently, without in any way tiring the voice.

As I have already explained, the muscles concerned with vocal sound are governed from the old, instinctive part of the brain; those concerned with speech, from that part of the brain which was last to develop. Working in harmony, the former provides the impulse, the mood, the emotional content; the latter, concerned with speech and with conscious thought, provides the intention, and should always lead. The more precise the thought, the more precise the articulation of the words, the more accurate and true will be the expression of feelings and emotions associated with those words. Without this precision, this truth of thought and feeling, a singer can never become an artist, an interpreter.

The Singer's Ear

This is a particularly difficult chapter to write, because it is one of the most difficult things that singers have to learn: to be guided by the ear, without falling into the error of listening to themselves 'from outside'. It is something intangible, but once experienced, once achieved, the results are most profound.

Singers must be able to learn from what they hear; from performances of the best singers, and from listening to music of all kinds. They must train their ears by listening intently, and consciously, to music. In particular they must acquire an acute awareness of harmony, of musical timbres, and phrasing. They must learn to apply this musical awareness to their singing. This training and conditioning of the ear, together with awareness of their own physical actions and reactions, are essential aspects of learning to sing.

Everyone's vocal habits and speech habits are conditioned by what is heard. When one listens to another singer, one responds not only to the sounds but, sympathetically, to the actions which produce those sounds. We all have the experience of feeling our own throats tighten in sympathy when listening to a tight-throated tenor. In the same way, a singer can be influenced very positively by listening to a healthy, well-produced voice.

They must, though, be careful not to fall into the trap of trying to imitate the actual sound of that voice. Every voice has its own personal and individual timbre, and any attempt to imitate the actual sound of someone else's voice leads into twofold danger. First, the imitators try to produce a sound which is not natural to them and which therefore cannot respond to their inner feelings and intentions. Secondly, they try to listen to themselves from outside, trying to control the result rather than the actions which produce that result.

Herein lies the danger of singers repeatedly listening to re-cordings, as an aide to memorization.

Such attempts, deliberate or not, to imitate the sound of someone else's voice, or to create a particular desired sound, result in unhealthy vocal tensions. (What singers hear of themselves is in any case a very distorted version of reality.) Such singers are interfering with the free response of their bodies to their musical, poetic, and dramatic imagination.

Singers must learn to know the difference between acute *awareness*, and *self-preoccupation*, which is perhaps the greatest enemy of communication, and therefore of good singing.

One of the most difficult things for any singer to learn, and one of the most important, is to be able mentally to hear the tones that they wish to sing before they are released into actual sound. Their ears must be acutely tuned to their *singing*; they must learn to be able to hear, but not to listen to their own *voice*. They must always be thinking forwards to what they are about to sing, not backwards to what they have just sung.

It is a matter of concentration; concentration on the music, and the harnessing of the imagination, *every time*, even when the music is just a single note or a simple scale. A singer must learn to use the inner ear—the ear of the imagination—and to trust the result.

As Lamperti said: 'Mentally anticipating internal sensa-tions of word, tone, and timbre, as well as interior activities that produce them, leads to control of the voice.'

But remember: it is impossible to be performer, audience, and critic at one and the same time.

The Pitch-Intensity Effect

In spite of my resolution to avoid strictly scientific matters in this book, there is one such subject which I feel I must touch on, which I believe to be of important significance for singers, and indeed for all practising musicians, and which for some reason is almost totally ignored. That is the 'pitch-intensity effect'; the fact that perceived pitch is not only a function of the frequency of tone, but also, under certain circumstances, and to a measurable extent, on its intensity, or loudness.

Many scientists have observed this phenomenon, but it was only first investigated fully by an American scientist, S. S. Stevens, who first published his findings as long ago as 1935, and again, in a book called *Hearing: Its Psychology and Physiology* published in 1938. Stevens's observations seem to me to be of such importance that I cannot understand why they are not more widely known. My attention was drawn to them by Professor Denis Fry, Professor of Phonetics at University College, London, himself incidentally an accomplished amateur singer.

Modern scientists have developed a far greater understanding of the phenomenon, but this is not the place to go into great scientific detail. I will try to explain the basic facts of Stevens's observations in simple terms.

It is generally accepted that the perceived pitch of a musical tone is a function of its frequency. What is not generally realized is that, in the case of a pure tone—that is a pure sine wave, a tone of given frequency without any harmonics or 'overtones'—the perceived pitch will also change with intensity, or loudness. In everyday musical practice of course, such 'pure' tones are rare but the effect can easily be observed with a tuning fork. A vibrating tuning-fork held close to the ear will appear to have a different pitch from the same fork held at a distance. (This has nothing to do with the 'Doppler effect', which involves change of pitch with movement.) The phenomenon can be demonstrated more easily, and dramatically, electronically.

In the region of 2,000 cycles per second (C above the soprano high C), the change of pitch with intensity is not significant, but at lower frequencies it is found that the perceived pitch drops progressively (by up to more than a third) with increasing intensity; the lower the frequency, the greater the effect. At frequencies higher than 2,000 cycles per second, on the other hand, the perceived pitch rises; the higher the frequency the greater the pitch variation. If, however, to a pure low frequency, overtones from the region above 2,000 cycles per second are added, the perceived pitch returns to 'normal', to what is expected.

This phenomenon is only fully apparent in the case of pure frequencies. If there is a full spectrum of harmonics, as is the case with a 'square wave', the effect disappears.

This has one obvious application. Traditionally orchestras have always tuned to an A given by the oboe—the instrument in the orchestra with the richest blend of harmonics—which ensures that all the members of the orchestra hear the same pitch, however far away they are sitting, however loud the sound may be.

It also explains why some singers, particularly those with a preponderance of low frequencies in their voice, can often, particularly when singing *mezza voce*, and omitting to add high frequencies to the spectrum of sound, appear to be singing under pitch. They believe themselves to be singing in tune, but the audience hears them as singing flat. I have often heard conductors say to bewildered singers: 'I am sure you believe yourself to be singing perfectly in tune, but *it sounds flat.*'

This is demonstrated very clearly in a simple exercise given by Alessandro Busti in his *Studio di canto* of 1865 (see Ex. 5). The diminuendo marked below the descending phrase indicates the natural reduction of the dynamics. The tendency will be, as the voice descends, for the proportion of low harmonics to increase. The crescendo above the line indicates that if the singer is still to sound in tune, there must be a

Ex. 5. Alessandro Busti, *Studio di canto*, exercise showing importance of increasing strength of high frequencies in descending passages

conscious increase in the higher frequency overtones of the harmonic spectrum.

We can, I am sure, all think of singers, sometimes world-famous singers, who have a tendency to sound under pitch whenever they lose the high harmonics from their voices. They seem to confuse dark, rich colour, and shadow. If they were made aware of the above phenomenon, and learned to maintain a high mixture of overtones (from the head-voice) in their vocal sound, this would not occur.

This is a further reason to support the old principle that the head-voice must always lead, and that concentration must always be maintained, if a singer's intonation is not to become very questionable.

Breath

As Sims Reeves wrote in his book *The Art of Singing*,

Cases are not infrequent where anatomical studies have a tendency to set up a sort of nervous dread in the singer that the breathing is not being done in the correct way. Incorrect breathing is an acquired habit, induced sometimes by an elaborate means taken to avoid it. A few simple hints are all that is necessary: the rest of what is called the art of breathing is very much a matter of instinct.

This may seem to be a gross simplification, but my own personal experience has done nothing to persuade me that Sims Reeves was wrong. Bad breathing habits are usually either acquired (often from the instructions of some 'breath faddist' teacher), the direct result of bad posture, or the result of the singer's inability to imagine the music in large.

It is essential, of course, for the singer's breathing apparatus to be in good working order. It is necessary, particularly at a time when bad postural and breathing habits are so widespread, to have exercises at our disposal which can help to ensure that this is so; but it is also important to realize that the sort of breathing designed specifically for exercising and developing the breathing apparatus is not the same as that needed for singing. There are many ways of breathing, appropriate to different human activities; and it is important that the breathing should adjust spontaneously to the activity in question. In ordinary quiet respiration, which can be observed in, say, a sleeping child, the breathing is predominantly what is called 'abdominal' (although of course it is nothing of the sort—the term 'abdominal breathing' indicates diaphragm breathing with minimal expansion of the ribs), whereas in vigorous, voluntary activities, such as singing, public speaking, athletic pursuits, or in a howling infant, intercostal and clavicular breathing also come into play. That means expanding and raising the chest. It was a well-established principle of the old school of singing, that only through the involvement of this thoracic breathing could resonance and flexibility be fully developed. It is no good trying to sing in a way which expresses strong emotions, or to run or jump, with breathing appropriate to meditation, or vice versa. A flexible, responsive breathing apparatus will react differently according to the demands made upon it. A deep, full breath, with the lungs filled to capacity, produces a feeling of fullness and stiffness which is not suitable for singing. The great Battistini went so far as to say that the longer the phrase he had to sing, the less breath he took, and 'never more than necessary to sniff the perfume of a tiny flower'. I assume that by this he meant that it was important on the one hand to avoid becoming overfull of air, and on the other hand, to remember that singing, including the control of the breath, is controlled from the *imposto*—associated with the parts of the airway leading to the organ of smell.

It is interesting to note the scorn with which so many writers on the subject of singing of an earlier period (when standards of singing are generally reckoned to have been very high) refer to 'modern' notions of abdominal breathing. Typical of many is that of Sir Charles Santley:

I have heard and read most amusing instructions for breathing, but, of all, I think 'abdominal breathing' is the most comical. I have in vain tried to discover whereabouts in the abdomen there exists a store-room for breath; wind there may be, perhaps, but not available for breathing purposes. I hope I do not incur any risk of an action for libel or hurt anybody's feelings in describing the authors of such theories as 'windbags'.

Elsewhere, he writes:

What [singers] ought to learn is to be able to take breath at any convenient point in a phrase in such a way that the break may not be observable. The lungs should never be entirely exhausted.... There is no mystery or difficulty about breathing. All it requires is care in arranging convenient and appropriate places to take breath, and practising speech or song accordingly.

In other words, breathing depends, to a large extent, on clear visualization and anticipation of what is to be sung if, as

I take it, Sir Charles Santley assumed that the singer maintained an habitually correct posture.

Dr George C. Cathcart, a distinguished London laryngologist who had in his youth studied singing with Scafarti in Naples, remembers

hearing Signor Scafarti say to a Bass whose voice he was trying: 'Voi respirate troppo basso, Signore'. [You are breathing too low]. This Bass had been trained in England to try and produce a low note by breathing as low as possible in the abdomen, whereas, Signor Scafarti was able to show him at the first lesson that he could get several lower notes by breathing high [with raised chest—not pushed up, but suspended from the back of the skull], and so causing his larynx to descend, than he could by breathing low and letting his larynx stay where it was.

My own experience of colleagues who have talked about 'pushing the breath down into the abdomen' is that although in some cases they achieved a certain sonority, in every case that I can recall, they lost flexibility and the ability to colour and modulate their voices; and their careers were almost invariably short.

All breathing involves the breathing muscle, the diaphragm; and the diaphragm works automatically if it is allowed to do so. Attempts to control breathing by stiffening the muscles of the midriff merely result in a blockage of energy. The control of breath is performed by the whole body, with the strength centred in the lower belly, and guided by the singer's intention, stimulated by imagination.

Esther Salaman gives very sound advice to singers: 'Never try to concentrate on what you think is your diaphragm—in fact it cannot be felt. You can, however, feel the breadth of the rib-cage and the braced area of the breast-bone, from whence a good deal of valuable resonance springs.'

The breath which 'falls into' the lungs as a result of a strong sudden pleasurable surprise is sufficient for the longest musical phrase that a singer is ever likely to encounter; this assumes that the phrase is clearly pictured in the imagination before the breath is taken, and that the concentration is maintained until the end.

If singers can sense their entire bodies as resonators, which need to be stimulated into vibration, rather than as bellows for blowing out air, then many of the 'problems' of breathing simply disappear. If they open up all the resonating cavities as part of the musical up-beat, and have a clear mental picture of the phrase to be sung, then sufficient air will fall into their lungs, automatically.

It is of course beneficial for singers to increase their vital capacity, and to be able to open up their chests, to maximize resonance and available oxygen; but exercises designed to assist this are not appropriate for the act of singing itself. Assuming (as always) an alert, balanced posture, *it is the impulse to sing which determines how we breathe*—which stimulates us to take breath appropriate to what is to be sung. The act of inhaling then happens as a result of the musical up-beat; it is an integral part of the musical phrase, and it should never be separated from it. The imaginative act that stimulates us to sing should therefore always take place *before* the intake of breath—not after. The intake of breath, and the preparation for singing, will then be in the character of the phrase which is about to be sung. (I am speaking here of the main breaths—not of small subsequent top-up breaths, which I will deal with later.)

One of the indications that a composer knows what he is about, when writing for the voice, is the extent to which he appreciates this, and makes such organic, musical breathing possible. Perhaps the greatest master in this respect is Handel. I can think of few places in his music where top-up breaths are really necessary. He seemed to know exactly how long a normal healthy singer could sustain a phrase. In this respect, as in almost every other, regular practice of Handel's vocal music can provide all the exercises a singer is likely to need. (I well remember, as a student, an old singer saying to me: 'You are a healthy young man. If you have to take a breath during a Handelian run, then you are probably singing it at the wrong speed. Now Bach is different; he didn't seem to care about such things.')

My conclusion is that the ability to sing long phrases, given a healthy breathing apparatus, and good physical and mental poise, is, to a very large extent, a matter of the singer's ability to *imagine* long phrases, to anticipate the pulse of the music, and to maintain mental (and consequently, physical) concentration.

Many singers have described what they call 'compressed breath'. This describes a well-known sensation, but is a misnomer. This feeling of compression is in fact that associated with keeping the ribs expanded, thereby preserving strong *negative* pressure in the pleurae (the spaces between the lungs and the ribs), which maintains the low sub-glottic pressure necessary for good vocal quality, and which allows for the spontaneous and quick descent of the diaphragm when air is needed for survival. But it is, above all, the feeling that comes from maintaining the whole being in the state of readiness; a state of expectant stillness, together with the joyful feeling associated with the desire to say something of tremendous importance.

There are many exercises designed to develop a healthy breathing apparatus, which can be of great benefit to singers. One of the clearest descriptions of such an exercise is to be found in Yogi Ramacharaka's book *The Hindu-Yogi Science of Breath*. He describes the Yogi Complete Breath as follows:

1) Stand or sit erect. Breathing through the nostrils, inhale steadily, first filling the lower part of the lungs, which is accomplished by bringing into play the diaphragm, which descending exerts a gentle pressure on the abdominal organs, pushing forward the front walls of the abdomen. Then fill the middle part of the lungs, pushing out the lower ribs, breast bone and chest. Then fill the higher portion of the lungs, protruding the upper chest, thus lifting the chest, including the upper six or seven pairs of ribs. In the final movement, the lower part of the abdomen will be slightly drawn in, which movement gives the lungs a support and also helps to fill the highest part of the lungs . . . The inhalation is continuous, the entire chest cavity from the lowered diaphragm to the highest point of the chest in the region of the collar bone, being expanded with a uniform movement. . . . Practice will soon overcome the tendency to divide the inhalation into three movements, and will result in a uniform continuous breath.

2) Retain the breath for a few seconds.

3) Exhale quite slowly, holding the chest in a firm position, and drawing the abdomen in a little and lifting it upward slowly as the air leaves the lungs. When the air is entirely exhaled, relax the chest and abdomen.

This exercise combines in one continuous movement, low (abdominal) breathing, mid- (intercostal) breathing, and high (clavicular) breathing. Exercising them all in this manner, develops a complete and healthy breathing apparatus, which is ready to react to the demands of singing when called upon to do so. But it is important to remember that this exercise is designed to improve the general condition of the breathing apparatus; it is not the specific breath for singing.

There is one exercise, similar to the above, that I would like to suggest. It is the only one that I ever personally used, and I have to say that as long as I paid attention to the basic simple principles of good posture, and maintained the *imposto* concentration, I never in forty-five years of professional singing had the slightest difficulty with breathing. I write as one who was lucky enough to be spared the attentions of teachers who might have persuaded me that it was a problem. As a teacher I have not yet met with a young singer whose breathing 'problems' did not solve themselves when *posture, impulse,* and *intention* were properly established. It is not so much a question of how much air you have at your disposal, but of how you dispose of it while singing. The body knows perfectly well how much breath it will need, if only you give it clear instructions as to what is expected.

I am aware that this sounds very simplistic; but this is deliberate. If breathing were as complicated a matter as some would have us believe, we would all have been dead long ago! In my own defence, I can only refer you again to the remarks of Sims Reeves, quoted at the beginning of this chapter.

The exercise is as follows:

1. In an easy, well-grounded stance, take a normal comfortably deep breath.
2. Without taking in more breath, raise and expand the chest, as when aroused or surprised.

3. Breathe out slowly and vigorously (blowing out on FF), without dropping the chest, or allowing it to collapse. This produces strong feelings in the lower abdomen and the loins.
4. Again without relaxing, or dropping the raised chest, release the abdomen, and observe how the air falls in instantaneously.
5. Repeat (3) and (4) several times.

One of the virtues of this exercise is that, through its practice singers can realize the speed with which the body can replenish itself with breath, automatically, if posture and attitude permit. They can realize that 'sucking in breath' is unnecessary, and, from their particular point of view, counter-productive. It will also help them to locate the feeling of strength in the lower belly, and loins.

The main purpose of the expanded chest is to create the optimum vibrating body, and to maintain the sucking effect of the pleurae on the lungs. The feeling of a low centre of gravity—of being well grounded—will enable the singer to avoid tension and energy blockage in the midriff.

The breathing appropriate to singing is that which is the natural result of being aroused or startled, without losing poise. The amount of breath inhaled is governed automatically by a concentrated visualization of the phrase to be sung. It is, or should be, in the end, as simple as that.

Lamperti said: 'A stereotyped manner of inhaling defeats the singer. Each phrase must 'take its own breath'. Olga Averino wrote: 'Avoid taking in air mechanically. This is essential . . . Since breath reflects our mental state, *take that breath to express the feeling of the musical phrase and text.* The emotional content will stimulate the impulse, and the impulse in turn will control the breath. If your desire to express the phrase is strong, and you feel the urge to sing it through to the very end, your breath control will be good.'

Sometimes, it is better for young singers to develop the ability to be observant, rather than always to accept instruction. I remember taking singing lessons from an Italian baritone; a really excellent singer, who had preserved his voice in perfect condition well into middle age. I asked him about posture and breathing.

T.H. [*Tapping my chest*] What do you do here, when you take a breath for singing?
ANSWER. Nothing, I let it hang.
T.H. [*Indicating my lower belly*]. What do you do here?
ANSWER. I push down.
T.H. Show me.
[*The baritone took a 'surprised' breath, raising his chest, drawing his lower abdomen in and up, and sang a beautiful, resonant, perfectly focused phrase.*]

He had in fact done exactly the opposite of what he had described. He had, I assume, answered my questions by simply repeating to me what he had read somewhere, or been told by some 'breath faddist'. His actual practice of singing was quite different—instinctive and 'correct'.

(I subsequently observed that the singers who had no common language with him, and simply copied him, had much greater benefit from his teaching than those with a good knowledge of Italian, who understood his instructions.)

There are three ways in which the singer should take in breath (always silently, with an open glottis):

1. The normal breathing of a well-poised, alert human being. Initiated simply by the body's need for oxygen. (During the periods when someone else is singing!)

2. The enhanced breathing of buoyant arousal, and concentrated preparedness for singing. Initiated by the musical or dramatic up-beat, and the *visualization of the phrase to be sung*. These main breaths are normally associated with new thoughts or new musical phrases, or simply with readiness to sing.

3. The little top-up breaths, in which small quantities of air 'fall into' the lungs. These are singers' punctuation marks, and of course their lifeline. Wherever possible these 'survival breaths' should be taken grammatically. When a composer knows his or her business, this 'wherever possible' should read 'always'. It is important here not to allow the chest to

fall, the 'instrument' to collapse, or to lose contact with the centre of gravity; to maintain concentration on the words and the music that is being sung, and *to think ahead*. It is essential that the vocal adjustment is not in any way changed by the act of taking these secondary breaths. It is amazing then, how long it is possible to continue to sing, with a series of small, inaudible, sustaining top-up breaths. If a singer becomes sufficiently adept, through practice, at taking these little breaths, the audience will be quite unaware of the breathing.

Over the years during the course of many singing classes, I have been amazed by the number of young singers who have never learned to take these little top-up breaths. They tend to overfill their lungs at the beginning, thereby losing all spontaneity and flexibility, and sing until they run out of breath, allow their instrument to collapse, wind it back up, take another huge gulp of air, and start the whole wearisome process all over again. This is usually the result of separating the act of breathing from the wish to make music. It is the singing equivalent of a violinist putting his instrument back in its case at the end of every phrase. It is the consequence of lack of sustained concentration and physical poise.

The taking of breath must never interrupt the flow of the music. Indeed, whenever the audience becomes aware of the singer taking breath, unless it is a breath taken for the purposes of dramatic expression, it is a sure sign that the singer has lost concentration on the song and has broken the 'magnetic thread' that holds the audience's attention; or it is a sign of bad planning—that the breath has been taken at inappropriate moments.

There are certain important rules which govern these top-up breaths:

1. They should be taken grammatically.
2. They should not be taken in the middle of a word; never, except for very special effects, between an adjective and its associated noun; never (especially important in German) between the parts of a compound noun or verb.

In florid music these rules do not necessarily apply. Here the rule is: if you have to take a top-up breath, then it should always be before a weak beat of the bar, not before a strong beat, and only in very exceptional circumstances at a barline. The time required for such breaths must always be taken from the end of the preceding note, never from the beginning of a note.

Also, if there are two alternative places to breathe, it is usually better to take the earlier alternative. Top-up breaths are much more difficult to execute, and sonority is always lost, if the reservoir is depleted.

One of the most frequent conversations that I have had during song-classes goes more or less as follows:

T.H. Why do you take so many breaths? Surely you can sing that whole phrase in one breath.

PUPIL. Oh no, I couldn't possibly do that.

T.H. Try.

[*Pupil tries, by taking an enormous breath, feels cramped, assumes an expression of the utmost panic, and fails.*]

T.H. Try not to suck in so much breath. Just give yourself a good up-beat, concentrate on the whole phrase, and try to have the end of the phrase in your mind from the very beginning.

[*Pupil sings the phrase in one breath.*]

PUPIL. Oh yes! It's much easier like that. But that is my problem, I am very short of breath. My teacher is working on it.

T.H. But you have just done it.

PUPIL. Yes I know; but that *is* my problem.

T.H. Try concentrating on the music instead of on your 'problem'. You could be in for a pleasant surprise.

I cannot repeat too often that long phrasing, and the manner of breathing which makes it possible, is largely a matter of concentration, and the ability to think in terms of whole phrases, rather than proceeding from note to note as if each note were a completely separate entity. Most of this work can be done silently.

I remember a recording session with the great Kirsten Flagstad. She had a very long phrase to sing and, no longer in her first youth, had decided that she should breathe somewhere in the middle of it. She said to the producer: 'I cannot decide where to breathe during this phrase.' The producer replied: 'My experience with really good singers is that if they are in any doubt about where to breathe, the answer is usually for them not to take a breath at all.' She tried it, and of course the producer had been right. The 'problem' had been entirely imaginary. She was of course a very great singer indeed. But the same rule applies to singers less bountifully endowed. It is, in the end, a matter of imagination, concentration, and courage. It is perhaps a truism, but I should remind my readers that such courage comes as a result of constant practice, and of, at some point, taking a risk.

Another memory of Flagstad: we rehearsed together one cold and damp morning, in an unheated rehearsal room. It was the sort of morning when one could see the breath coming from the mouths of the singers. Everyone had a little visible puff of vapour in front of their mouths as they sang— usually about 10–15 cm. long. But in Flagstad's case, the vapour apeared to linger in front of her mouth, not more than 2–3-cm., and almost to be reinhaled into her nose as she sang. The air was in fact virtually still, as in the old exercise of singing without disturbing the flame of a lighted candle, held in front of the mouth. Flagstad gave a wonderful example of what Charles Lunn wrote in 1904, in his book *The Voice*:

Voice is not a matter of letting out air (breath), but air waves (vibrations), which do not require a current of air to carry them along any more than rings in a pond from a fallen stone require a current of water to enable them to reach the edge of the pond.

Later, Lunn writes:

We are material, animal and spiritual. If the higher or spiritual side rule the lower or animal side, then we are artists; if the lower or animal side rule the higher or spiritual side of our natures, then we are *mere performers*. As animals we must breathe. If we breathe when we sing because we must, then our lower or animal side rules, but if we breathe because we choose, then our higher or spiritual nature rules. From the beginning of study enlist the mind.

One word to young singers:

> If you have no problem with breathing, if your breathing apparatus responds automatically to the demands made upon it by your instinct for singing, and if you can alert your body without becoming tense, then do not allow breath faddists to interfere with that natural coordination by creating unhealthy self-consciousness. Just remember: when singing, we do not breathe *in order* to sing; we breathe *because* we sing. And we sing because our imaginations, our feelings, and our souls demand it.

PART III
Words and Music

The Work of the Imagination: The Study of Vocal Music

I have already stated the theme-song of this book:

> Imagination is an essential prerequisite of singing—not an optional extra.

The purpose, indeed the sole purpose, of training for the profession of singing is to improve the connection between the imagination and the sounds that eventually issue from the singer's mouth. The more competent the singer, the closer will be that connection, and therefore the greater the extent to which the quality of the end-result will depend on the quality of the imaginative activity that initiated the whole process.

I would like to remind you of the words of Sir Charles Santley's teacher, Gaetano Nava, who 'insisted that the object of music was to give greater expression and emphasis to the words'. Here he agreed with Gluck's librettist Ranieri de' Calzabigi, who wrote in a letter to Count Kaunitz about his and Gluck's plan for *Alceste*: 'The music has no other function than to express what arises from the words.'

This is not in any way meant to minimize the importance of the music, but simply to reaffirm the indissoluble connection between words and music; to remind us that the music written for singing, and also the manner of singing, must always be appropriate to the thoughts and feelings expressed in the text.

Too often this is forgotten by singers, at least until the last moment of their preparatory work, when they attempt to add text, feeling, and expression, after long periods devoted entirely to mechanical vocalizing, divorced from imagination. The result, too often, is that we hear singing which, though possibly healthy, mellifluous, or forceful enough, is only related to the content of what is sung in the most superficial and generalized way.

With very rare exceptions, it is the words, and the ideas contained in those words, that inspire the composer to write music which gives them greater expression and emphasis; even music that sometimes temporarily takes over from the words, as in passages of coloratura or fioritura—pure vocal expressiveness. Therefore any approach to the interpretation of vocal music, be it in the form of songs, oratorios, or operas, must of necessity begin with consideration of the text which has been set to music. This need not be great poetry. Indeed, the greatest poetry, containing as it does its own 'music'—poetry in which the actual sound of the words plays a very important part—is often unsuited to musical composition. Why otherwise are there so few musical settings of Shakespeare's sonnets? (As opposed to the songs from his plays, which are always written in a much simpler style.) Only a very brave, or even foolhardy, composer would feel that he had much to add to the music of, for example, Keats's Odes.

The ideas and the sentiments contained in the poetry, together with its form and rhythm, are the basis of the music which the composer has written, to add expressiveness and understanding, to communicate the feelings associated with the words, to flesh them out. The initial germ of the song, the imaginative stimulus, is contained in the poem. This is not to suggest that the poem is more important than the music; simply that in vocal music it is always an essential component, and almost invariably came before the music, as the expression of the initial concept. The great operatic composers have always taken the greatest pains to get their librettos right, even when their purely literary merit has not been significant. No composer worth his or her salt would write a song unless there were something in the poetry which stimulated their imagination, and which inspired them to set it to music; either in its form or its content—preferably both.

This is as true in the case of an operatic aria by Bellini or an oratorio aria by Bach as it is in the case of a song by Benjamin

Britten or Hugo Wolf. Of course, Hugo Wolf gives much more importance to the small details of musical word-setting than does Bellini. But the general rule still applies: until singers know what the poet is saying, they cannot be in a position to make their singing appropriate to the poetry, and to the dramatic situation; accurately appropriate to the sentiments being expressed. They cannot interpret the music in anything but the most generalized and superficial way.

Every work of art has both form and content. While it is often possible to know the *form* of a song, or an aria, in a general way, from the music alone, it is not possible to know its *content* without an understanding—a detailed understanding—of the words.

It is all too easy to misinterpret the music of a song, if its contents have not been clearly established. When Beethoven, wishing to increase his income (and that of his publisher), agreed to make arrangements for the domestic, amateur market, of Scottish folksongs, he was sent a collection of melodies to work on, but without the accompanying words. His arrangements, while in themselves pleasant enough, were often completely wide of the mark—even to the extent that one song which was originally a lullaby emerged as a vigorous battle-song. Another example can be found in the gentle lilting French Christmas song 'Quelle est cette odeur agréable', which appears as a hearty drinking-song, 'Fill every glass', in the *Beggar's Opera*.

An instrumentalist, presented with the melody and rhythm of a piece of music, has the freedom to perform it with a very wide range of different expression. If harmony is added, then already the range of possible interpretations is greatly limited; because harmony, the language of emotion, already indicates the mood and the associated feelings. If the music is combined with words, then the range of possible appropriate musical interpretations is once more reduced.

It is often possible to interpret a poem in a number of different ways; but a singer-interpreter must always respect the fact that the composer has already declared his hand by writing music which is appropriate to *his* own understanding

of that poem. Singers are not free to give an individual interpretation of a poem, while ignoring what the composer has
done; nor free to sing the composer's music, while ignoring
the words which make clear the thoughts and feelings of
which that music is an expression. The great composers of
vocal music have usually left sufficiently clear indications
as to their understanding of, and their feelings about, the
poem; singers' concern must be to use their imagination to try
to understand those indications. Only when this has been
done can they consider themselves free, within proper para-
meters, to make their own individual contribution to the
performance.

Because of the music, then, singers are less free than actors
would be in deciding on their interpretation of the words; and
because of the words, they are less free than an instrumentalist in their interpretation of the music. But within the bounds
of these restrictions, the opportunities for expression are immense, because they have both words and music, and the
infinite subtleties of their combination and interplay, at their
disposal.

This applies equally to accompanists, conductors, and operatic stage directors. One of the most frustrating experiences
that a singer has to contend with, is to be involved in an opera
production with a musically insensitive director. A warning
signal is often given when the director arrives at rehearsal
with a copy of the libretto but no musical score. A theatre
director, used to the freedom of being able to interpret the
words in his own way, often finds it difficult to accept the fact
that the composer has already given his own particular interpretation of those words.

Of course, a director who tried to work from the music
alone, while ignoring the words would be equally misguided.

I can think of all too many examples of the first category,
from my own experience. One particularly blatant example
that comes to mind was a famous, successful, but unmusical
theatre director, who had been engaged to direct Mozart's
Così fan tutte. He had decided that the words of Dorabella's
second-act aria should be interpreted as a bitter and militant

feminist declaration of resentment at men, and the whole business of love.

Love is a little thief, a serpent who gives peace to our hearts, or takes it away, just as he pleases. No sooner has he opened a path to our hearts, through the eyes, than he puts the spirit in chains, and deprives it of freedom . . .

I suppose it would be possible, even reasonable, in a play, to deliver such lines in a spirit of aggressive resentment. But just look at the music that Mozart has written for those words (see Ex. 6). Every note declares that Dorabella is happy with the effects that love has on her. She is saying, as it were: 'In spite of all the difficulties of love, isn't it fun! isn't is wonderful!' The charming, light-hearted, dancing, tune shows, in every bar, Dorabella's happy, if perhaps, in the middle section, somewhat rueful, acceptance of the situation. She has fallen in love, and that, despite the problems it may bring, is really all that counts. The poor singer who was expected to distort this charming bubbly little song into

Ex. 6. Mozart, 'È amore un ladroncello', from *Così fan tutte*, Act 2

Dorabella

Allegretto vivace

È a - mo - re un la - dron - cel - lo, un

ser - pen - tel - lo è a - mor, _____ ei

to - glie e dà la pa - ce, la

pa - ce co - me gli pia - ce ai cor.

something aggressive and resentful, was forced by the director to try and give it expression totally contrary to the feeling
expressed in the music. Her performance of course, was not,
nor could it possibly have been, a success. An aria which
clearly demands a certain happy frivolity of expression, with
lyrical quality adjustment, with definite joyful mood, and a
slight move towards the OO mood in the middle section, was
spoiled by the singer's having to attempt to sing the song
with too dramatic a quality, and with too much aggression in
the mood. She sang it very well, but in a manner which,
though conceivably appropriate to the words, was quite inappropriate to the composer's clearly stated interpretation of
them.

Such situations are by no means rare. But, just as singers
must accept certain limitations on their freedom, so should
directors, conductors, and accompanists. This limitation
should be seen not as something to be ignored or overcome,
but as a welcome challenge to their artistic imaginations.
Simply 'doing something different' is just too easy, is usually
indicative of lack of true imagination, and the excuse too
often of the arrogant and lazy.

How different from the approach of the great director Carl
Ebert who, when he first directed operas, always had his
musical assistant by his side, making sure that what he asked
the singers to do dramatically was in accordance with the
composer's intentions as expressed in the music. No wonder
this assistant, young Berthold Goldschmidt, was given the
nick-name 'Ebert's right ear'.

A singer, in order to be able to interpret vocal music,
whatever form it may take, must come as close as possible to
the composer's intentions when the music was written. The
proper use of the imagination is not to wonder 'what can I
do with this song?', but in the first place, to do everything
possible to try and understand why the composer has written
it as he has done. Only then can the singer's own individual
contribution properly be brought to the performance.

Having once decided that the music is suited to his or her
vocal range and character, and having formed a general pic-

ture of the song 'in the rough', then the singer's work should always commence with a careful study of the text. As Sims Reeves wrote:

The person who does not recite the verses of a song aloud, as an exercise in pronunciation, before attempting the music, will never become a perfect artist.

Sergius Kagen wrote to the same effect:

A singer who cannot recite a song text with proper conversational inflection (that is, in a manner where the logic of the sentence is clearly presented to the listener, where punctuation is observed, where words of greater importance received greater emphasis) cannot hope to learn to phrase a song. Phrasing of most vocal music is based upon the meaning of a sentence, and its effect upon the inflection with which one recites this sentence and sings the corresponding musical part.

Manuel García junior, in his *Hints on Singing* (1894) wrote:

The pupil must read the words of the piece again and again till the finest shadow of meaning has been mastered. He must next recite them with perfect simplicity and self-abandonment. The accent of truth apparent in the voice when speaking naturally is the basis of expression in singing. Light and shade, accent, sentiment, all become eloquent and persuasive. The imitation of instinctive impulse must, therefore be the object of this special preparation.

García is not suggesting that singing is merely an extension of speech, but that if singing is to be meaningful, the meaning must be based on the words that are sung. 'Expression' is a meaningless concept unless it is quite clear what it is that is to be expressed. The composer began with the text, and so must the singer.

It is often recommended to young singers that they should start to study a song by learning the melody, and vocalizing on a single vowel-sound. This all-too-common practice is responsible for a great deal of bland, generalized singing. It is also to a large extent responsible for the erroneous belief on the part of singers that diction is incompatible with beautiful singing. If from the very beginning of study, the text and the meaning are ignored, or put firmly into the back of the singer's mind, that is where they will always, to a certain extent, remain. All attempts to bring the text out of its obscurity will tend to be seen as an intrusion, an interference with the process of vocalization. Sometimes, certainly, it is helpful to vocalize in this manner, but only at a much later stage of the study, and then only in order to deal with very special problems—these problems frequently having their origin either in lazy, imprecise articulation of consonants, or in failure to distinguish between vowels of phonation and vowels of articulation—between mood and diction. It is a practice which can be useful, but only *after* the words have already been firmly fixed in the singer's memory and imagination, and when the lips, the palate, and the forward part of the tongue, already have the 'feel' of the words well established.

The problem with vocal exercises, is that often too much time is spent by young singers in activity that they will not be called upon to perform in practice. The coloratura passages in, say, 'Rejoice greatly' from Handel's *Messiah* are significantly different when practised on an AA vowel, from the same passages sung on the word 'rejoice', with that word, and its meaning held in mind throughout. Arthur Cranmer went so far as to recommend young singers never to exercise on vowel-sounds divorced from text. An exercise sung on the word 'large' will immediately involve the imagination, whereas the same exercise sung simply on AA can too easily become merely mechanical.

In my experience, singers who start by vocalizing, and then try to add the words later, rarely achieve the clear, imaginative declamation of the text that all vocal music requires. The accurate and subtle matching of vocal tone to the sentiments to be expressed will probably never be fully realized. All too often, the text, seen as an unwelcome imposition, is treated in a slovenly manner; and in the process the singers have denied themselves, and their audience, the expressive possibilities of the poem which provided the initial inspiration for the composer. They will have surrendered to the easy lure of generalization. Also they will deny themselves the assistance that clear diction gives in establishing a good focus for the vocal sound.

The further danger is, that the singer who, having first vocalized the melody, wishes to 'make something of the words', will proceed to exaggerate them, distorting both words and, as a result of excessive jaw movements, the purely vocal elements. In fact this all-too-common practice of vocalizing first and adding the words later is almost always, in the end, counter-productive. If the natural and logical sequence I have described is followed, then each element can more easily take its proper place in the scheme of things.

The purpose of studying a song is not to 'hang' the contents of the song on to the singers' voices, and what they choose to call their 'technique', but to bring that technique to bear on the contents of the song. The implication of this must surely be that a singer's first priority should be to establish as detailed an understanding of those contents as possible. It is not enough to have a general idea of what the song is about. Generalization and approximation lead to mediocrity, the enemy of all art.

Caccini, one of the principal founders of post-Renaissance solo singing, in the preface to *Le nuove musiche* (1602) wrote that many faults of singing 'Lie in the musician's not really having mastered beforehand the matter he wishes to sing; for if he had, unquestionably he would not fall into such errors. This art admits of no mediocrity, and the more delightful the qualities we may find in it, the more must we bestir ourselves to bring them out with enthusiasm and love.'

Imagination must lead; and if it is to have something real to work on, it must start with the words. Those words, arising from the original concept, have acted as a stimulus to the composer's imagination, and the composer has given expression to them in several different ways.

1. By taking the natural rhythm and inflexion of the text, often giving special rhythmic emphasis to particular words.

2. By highlighting the words felt to be specially important, through the characteristics of the melodic line and the harmony, sometimes giving special emphasis to certain words by extending them with fioritura and passages of coloratura.

3. By creating, with music, the special atmosphere felt to be associated with the poem, and by trying to establish as clearly as possible the character and the mood; but these things can only be indicated. It is the singer's responsibility to decide what voice quality and what mood are best suited to the poem as set to music by the composer.

The composer has created the architectural framework of the song, the aria, or the opera, which gives form and coherence to all the above details. This involves both the phrasing and the harmony. Without a disciplined understanding of, and feeling for, this architectural aspect, the singer's attempts to be 'interesting' can all too easily degenerate into mere self-indulgent mannerisms.

Work on the Text

Work on the text involves consideration of:

1. meaning;
2. the basic rhythm and pulse;
3. the sound of the words;
4. where new thoughts arise.

MEANING

This is particularly important in the case of texts in foreign languages. It is not enough to read through a vernacular version—which more often than not is a free translation, and can be very misleading. Every word must be understood, and both its meaning and its sound thoroughly mastered and relished.

At this stage it should be possible to answer the following simple questions:

What is the poet saying, and why?
Who is singing?
To whom is the singer singing?
What is the mood? What is the atmosphere?

What is the poet saying, and why?

What is the content of the text? Is the singer telling a story, or describing a scene? or expressing private thoughts? or praying, or meditating? What emotions are being expressed? Is it a scene with different characters which is being enacted? Just what is it all about?

The singer must, in fact, *classify* the song. This is not necessarily to suggest that all songs fall into one of a selection of clear-cut classifications. But if singers are to be clear in their minds about the general nature of what they are trying to communicate to an audience, it is essential to give answers to the above questions.

Harry Plunket Greene suggests the following rough categories:

1. Atmospheric
2. Dramatic
3. Narrative
4. Songs of Characterization
5. Songs of Reminiscence
6. Contemplative
7. Songs of Address or Ode Songs
8. Bel canto, Florid, and Rhythmical
9. Ghost Songs
10. Songs of Question and Answer
11. Humorous and Quasi-humorous
12. Folksongs

The lists of examples that he gives in his book makes it clear that such classification is very much a matter of individual choice. But this fact does not absolve singers from deciding for themselves, at the very beginning of their study, what sort of song they are dealing with.

In the case of an opera, or of a song cycle with a dramatic story-line, it is important to know everything possible about the dramatic situation, and to be aware, while singing, of everything that the particular character who is singing can know about the situation, in each song, *up to that moment.*

Some of the worst distortions of interpretation in my experience come from well-meaning singers who, knowing the end of the story, lose all immediacy in the reliving of the early stages. The tears of joy in the early songs of Schumann's *Dichterliebe* become distorted into tragic tears, because the singer knows that a few songs later, the young lover will be rejected. This is usually justified on the grounds of 'premonition'. Such specious premonition destroys the immediacy of the emotions expressed in those early songs. Overpowering happiness can, after all, also result in tears, even in recollection, if sufficiently vivid; indeed any sudden new emotion can do so. If the composer, with a momentary harmonic tug at the heartstrings in the accompaniment, chooses to indicate that *he* knows what is afoot, that is a different matter. The fact that the singer is reliving the experience of early happiness only makes that harmonic tug more poignant. It is not necessary—not appropriate—for the singer to indicate that he knows it too. (To those who justify the above dramatic distortion on the grounds that the singer is remembering the situation, I would point out that, apart from the very first introductory song, all the poems are in the present tense. The singer is in fact *reliving* the whole story; hence the dramatic directness of the songs.) Sometimes, however, a composer will write accompaniments which express different feelings from those of the singer. I think for example of the song 'Mein Liebster singt' in Hugo Wolf's *Italienisches Liederbuch*, where the accompaniment provides the lover serenading outside the house, while his mistress expresses her frustration at not being able to join him.

Who is singing?

Is it a clearly defined character, as in an opera? Is it perhaps simply 'the poet'? What do we know about this character? Light-hearted and rather frivolous, or serious and introspective? Young and naïve, or perhaps an older and more experienced man or woman of the world? Is this character gentle and sensitive, or a passionate extrovert? a down-to-earth peasant or a member of the elegant society? a romantic ideal-ist? or just sexy? or both? How old is this person? (It is important to remember that many songs express the thoughts and feelings of young people. We are so used to hearing some songs sung by middle-aged prima donnas or well-rounded, self-satisfied baritones, that we tend to forget this fact.)

The answer to this question is important in choosing the right *voice quality*. As a general rule, lightweight characters require light voice quality. Dramatic quality should be reserved for the expression of deep emotional involvement, and is most often called for in dramatic music. Light and lyrical qualities, with slight shifts to one side or another, are the ones which prove most generally useful in the song repertoire, in pre-nineteenth-century music, and with notable exceptions such as Verdi's Requiem or Janáček's *Glagolitic Mass* in oratorio.

In general, voice quality, expressing the character of the singer, should remain constant throughout a song, with the obvious exception of songs where the singer is required to portray more than one character, as in, say, Schubert's 'Erlkönig'.

To whom is the singer singing?

This is sometimes obvious from the text, particularly in opera; but by no means always so. If singing is a form of communication, there must be not only a communicator, but also someone with whom he or she is communicating. Is it the world at large? is it God? is it a friend? is it a distant lover? or a lover who is close at hand? is it a hated enemy? is it the audience, directly? Is the singer perhaps singing to him- or herself? Whatever the answer to this question, the audience must, of course, also always be included. Singers must always share their experiences with the audience; that is why they are there.

What is the mood? What is the atmosphere?

How are we to define atmosphere? Surely we can only do that in terms of the mood that is engendered in the singer by the scene or the situation which has inspired the text and the music, and which is something objective. A red sunset has, of itself, no atmosphere; that comes from the poet's and the composer's subjective reaction. Singers must re-create, in their imagination, the situation that gave rise to the poetry and the music, and they must react to that situation, and thereby communicate the atmosphere, by singing.

The range of mood is virtually infinite, but as I have explained in the chapter 'Colour', above, it is possible to be more precise about this than is often realized. If singers have trained themselves to respond vocally to different moods with clarity and accuracy, they can allow themselves to be guided by intuition and imagination. But they must know what mood they are expressing, if they are to avoid on the one hand mere bland vocalization, or on the other hand, imposed 'colouring'—or caricature. If they have simply trained themselves to produce 'their sound', then the only means at their disposal are changes of dynamics and verbal distortion. (Their individual vocal timbre will be there anyway, unless it has been obliterated by too much mechanistic training.) The singer in such cases is giving us a description of the song, rather than sharing with us the dramatic, poetic, musical, emotional, physical experience which brought the song into existence. The listeners then may respond with their ears, but are not touched in their deepest feelings.

Very often, the dramatic situation of the singer of a song, seen objectively, is different from what the character is momentarily feeling. The singer in Beethoven's *An die ferne Geliebte* is melancholy, because he misses his far-off beloved. But in section two of the cycle, when he expresses his longing to be with her, he actually imagines the happiness of their being together, and it is that imagined happiness which should determine the principal mood expressed in the colour of the singer's voice. If the singer can combine this with a feeling of longing, without changing the main mood, then the song becomes doubly poignant.

When the imagination is strong enough and the singer responsively alert, the body does not distinguish between the imagination and 'reality'. If the young boy in the song imagines for a moment that he is actually with his beloved, he will react as though this were really true. This aspect of interpretation is often misunderstood. Reliving an experience in the imagination causes similar physical reactions to those caused by the original experience. (Try to recall a really happy experience, in all its details, without at the same time smiling!) This is the basis of all modern 'visualization therapy'. It is, traditionally, the basis of all good singing habits.

Schubert showed his understanding of this in his song 'Frühlingstraum' (see Ex. 7). The three sections of each verse indicate:

(a) Genuine experience of happiness (even if in a dream).
(b) The shock of a rude awakening to present reality.
(c) The reflecting on the real-life situation.

If the first section is sung in any mood other then real happiness, the other two sections become less true, and the whole song sentimentalized.

One classic example of this is Richard Strauss's song 'Allerseelen'. The poet is remembering the happiness of young love, and feels intense longing for its return. The fact that he has in the mean time lost his love should not colour the song to the extent that what is, after all, a rapt lovesong full of longing, should be turned into a dirge, as is so very often the case. To say 'Wouldn't it be wonderful if . . .' with the gloomy, doom-laden tone sometimes assumed by singers of this song reduces it to complete nonsense. The two staccato notes at the end of the second bar of the accompaniment would sound intolerably frivolous if the song were really as gloomy as some people seem to imagine! (See Ex. 8.)

Is the character in the poem perhaps describing a scene? In which case, who is doing the describing? It is important, even if the song or part of a song is descriptive, to decide just who it is giving the description, and what part, if any, they play in the dramatic situation; what is the observer's attitude to what is happening?

Consider Richard Strauss's song 'Schlechtes Wetter'. The

Ex. 7. Schubert, 'Frühlingstraum', from *Die Winterreise*, D911: verse 1

Ex. 7. *Continued*

Ex. 7. *Continued*

Ex. 7. *Continued*

an den Fen - ster-schei - ben, wer mal - te die Blät - ter da? Ihr lacht wohl ü - ben den Träu - mer, der Blu - men im Win - ter sah, der Blu - men im Win - ter sah?

singer-observer looks out on a cold snowy evening, and sees her neighbour going out shopping. What is her attitude to the young girl sitting at home with her feet up, while her mother goes out into the cold, wet night to fetch the materials for baking a cake for her? Does she think the girl to be very

Ex. 8. Richard Strauss, 'Allerseelen', Op. 10 No. 8

Ex. 8. *Continued*

Tisch die duf-ten-den Re - se - den, die

letz - ten ro - ten A - stern trag' her - bei,

fortunate, or does she think her a fat lazy good-for-nothing? Does she pity the mother for being so abused by her daughter? or does she admire her for being so sweet and kind to the girl? Is she envious of the girl, or is she disgusted? If the singer decides that she, as observer, is quite happy about the situation—simply thinks that it is a pity it is such bad weather—then she must use quite a different mood from the one she would choose if she thinks badly about the girl and the whole situation. In this case, a move slightly towards the aggressive mood would seem appropriate. On the other hand, it might be possible to consider the observer as being quite detached and neutral in her feelings. In that case why would Strauss have bothered to write the song, or the poet to write the poem? A brief look at the music would, I think, quickly dismiss that idea. I recently heard this song, sung by a very well-known soprano who had quite obviously not thought about any of these questions. The resulting performance was 'pretty', but, as far as I could hear, quite meaningless.

One thing I should add at this point: frequently, during the course of song-classes, I have asked a singer what mood he or she is trying to express, and have been given the answer 'depressed'. This is *never* a good answer; it always results in boredom for the listeners. The character who is singing may be sad, or deeply troubled, but not depressed. When depressed, one does not sing! Depression involves a lack of vital energy, whereas singing always demands an abundance of energy, even when expressing the depths of sadness; even, perhaps especially, when expressing a state of blissful spiritual calm.

THE BASIC RHYTHM, AND PULSE

This is where the process of reading the poem aloud becomes so important. The poem must be thoroughly absorbed, and spoken with the rhythm and phrasing given to it by the composer. It must be decided which words need highlighting (not necessarily stressing), and which words can be given less weight. This study of the prosody is the first stage in understanding the composer's interpretation of the poem. I write at greater length about the pulse in a later chapter. Very often, composers repeat words, or even whole phrases of the text. Singers should be aware that this repetition must always be motivated. In general, it is done for one of two reasons: the composer wishes to intensify the feelings expressed first time round, or, having expressed the feelings associated with the words very strongly first time, seeks to internalize those feelings—sometimes even to meditate on what has just been said. Never should they be treated as simple aimless repetition.

THE SOUND OF THE WORDS

The clear pronunciation, and awareness of the poet's use of vowel-sounds, alliterative consonants, and rhyme-schemes, if indeed these play a part in the poem.

Consider Vaughan Williams's well-known song 'The Vagabond'.

> B-r̲-ight is the r̲-ing of words
> When the r̲-ight man r̲-ings them;
> F̲-air the f̲-all of s̲-ongs
> When the s̲-inger s̲-ings them.

or the heroic *frisson* given to Wolfram's address in the second act of Wagner's *Tannhäuser*:

> So viel der Helden,
> He-r̲r̲-lich, f-r̲-isch und g-r̲-ün.

AWARENESS OF WHERE NEW THOUGHTS ARISE

New thoughts usually mean new anacruses; often a new main breath, a new mood, a new physical adjustment of balance which must be sustained throughout the expression of this new thought. This is particularly important in *recitative*. Mozart provides the perfect model here. Invariably, in his music, a new thought is associated with a new harmony. (This is why it is a dangerous practice to make cuts in Mozart's recitatives. Too often, making cuts involves modulating in the middle of a thought—something that Mozart himself never does, and which always sounds 'wrong'.)

At this stage, the words should be memorized, so that they can be thoroughly digested, and so that the singer does not have to worry about remembering them. In fact, by the time all the above work has been done, the singer will usually find that he has already to a very large extent memorized the text. Much of a singer's best work can, and should be done silently; mentally declaiming the words of the song, while walking perhaps, or while waiting at a bus stop, or sitting in a train, can be of enormous benefit in the preparation of any vocal music. As Tosi wrote: 'Singing requires so strict an

Application, that one must study with the Mind, when one cannot with the Voice.'

Now, and only now, comes the time to learn the music.

Work on the Music

This involves consideration of:

1. the general shape of the music;
2. word-setting;
3. the accompaniment;
4. musical detail.

The General Shape of the Music

Particular attention should be given to the underlying harmonic structure of the music. This does not require a detailed theoretical analysis of the music; simply that the singer must be aware how the music moves from one harmony to another; from one thought to another; from one feeling to another; from one mood to another. In the case of composers who know their business, of whatever period, the general rule

New thought = New anacrusis and New harmony

is almost invariably followed.

This skill is best developed with music from the earlier period of classic song, when harmonic movement was in general much slower and clearer, and when thoughts and moods changed less hectically than at later times.

Word-setting

This is the special meaning given to individual words and phrases by the composer, through rhythmic, melodic, and harmonic colour and passing modulation. As a general rule, the broader the scale of the music, the more it modulates according to whole phrases, whole sections, rather than to particular words.

To take an example from the literature of German song, Franz Schubert, who was closer in time to the period of the *concerto grosso*, and the harpsichord, when colour changes could only take place between phrases, or paragraphs, almost invariably makes his colour changes in this way—from phrase to phrase, from paragraph to paragraph, not from word to word; whereas Hugo Wolf, influenced by Wagner, frequently demands changes of colour and harmony between individual words. The modern tendency to sing Schubert's songs as though they had been composed by Hugo Wolf can only be deplored, however skilled or famous the perpetrators.

The Accompaniment

This is an integral part of the music, which often gives essential clues to the singer as to how the song should be sung, and which must be studied and thoroughly absorbed.

Musical Detail

On the first day of the First Bayreuth Festival in 1876 Richard Wagner put up copies of a notice throughout the Festival Theatre which said, among other things:

Last request
to my faithful artists!
Distinctness. The big notes will look after themselves;
the little notes,
and the words are the things to watch.

A glance at any page of the score of an opera by Wagner, will show what he meant. The vocal line is full of detail, which, if once understood and absorbed, provides the singer with virtually all the clues needed for the characterization.

Let us look at the entry of Pogner and Beckmesser in Act 1 of Wagner's *Die Meistersinger von Nürnberg*, in which Beckmesser in particular reveals virtually every side of his complicated character, through the words, and the musical detail, rendering caricature quite unnecessary. (See Ex. 9.)

Ex. 9. Wagner, *Die Meistersinger von Nürnberg*, Act 1: entry of Pogner and Beckmesser

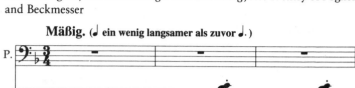

Ex. 9. *Continued*

Ex. 9. *Continued*

Ex. 9. *Continued*

al - len Din - gen sollt euch an dem ge - le - gen

poco cresc. _ _ _ _ _ _ _ _ _ _ _ _ _

sein?   Könnt ihr der Toch - ter Wunsch   nicht

mf   *p*

zwin - gen,   wie   mög - tet ihr wohl um sie

più p

Ex. 9. *Continued*

ation*   141

Ex. 9. Continued

Bars 13–15 Precise, angular, pedantic, nervous.
Bars 16–17 Exaggerated legato—insinuating.
Bar 18   Proud, vain—expressed with the acciacciatura.

Then later:

Bars 26–7   Nervous, irritated.
Bars 27–31 Subservient, slimy.
Bars 32–3   Artificially jovial.
Bars 34–7   Suspicious.

Throughout, Pogner sings with consistent, harmonious, confident legato.

It is my contention that composers are no more willing than most people, to waste their energies on unnecessary activity. If therefore a composer takes the trouble to write a small detail into a vocal line, the singer should assume that there was a good reason for doing so. Frequently, tiny details provide keys which can open doors into the mind of the composer. Even if in performance, when a singer is able to conceive of his song 'in large', such details are not consciously heard by the majority of the audience, they can still, if properly digested during the period of study, have a significant effect on the singer's approach to the song. Small details should not be dwelt upon or overemphasized in performance; that can lead to pedantry, self-consciousness, and lack of spontaneity. But if singers are to avoid either bland mediocrity, or generalized emotional self-indulgence, then they must spend time, effort, and imagination, in trying to understand and interpret for themselves the significance of all the details. Again and again, the changing or ignoring of a small detail can change the character of a whole phrase, or even a whole song. I repeat, it is not for the sake of the details themselves, but for the sake of the key they provide to the composer's intentions.

Over the years, one of the most common observations I have found myself making, in the course of song-classes, is: 'That is very fine, but if the composer had actually wanted you to give the phrase that particular expression, he would surely have written it differently.'

Or, when a young singer says: 'I'm not sure what to do with this passage', the answer most often has to be: 'Try following the composer's instructions! Also if a composer who is in the habit of writing down many detailed instructions, writes a passage with no instructions at all, have the courage to try just singing it as simply as you can.'

To take, at random, one small example, which I have so very often heard ignored: the song 'Benedeit' from Hugo Wolf's *Italienisches Liederbuch*. The first phrase reads 'Benedeit die sel'ge Mutter, die so lieblich dich geboren' (see Ex. 10*a*). The obvious thing might be to make the whole of this phrase a single smoothly executed statement: 'Blessed be the happy mother who bore you so lovingly', and this is how I have often heard it sung, with a breath taken after 'Mutter'. But Wolf phrased it differently, and less obviously. He has separated the word 'Benedeit' from the rest of the phrase, by inserting a quaver rest. By going against the obvious, he has surely indicated that he wants that word to be given special significance. The word 'Benedeit' must be highlighted—not emphasized, stressed, or exaggerated but, as it were, given a halo. It is as though the singer feels the need to cross himself as he sings that one special word. To ignore, or to gloss over,

Ex. 10. Wolf, 'Benedeit die sel'ger Mutter', from *Italienisches Liederbuch*

that short silence is to reduce the first phrase of the song to a mere statement, instead of its being a declaration of elevated, almost holy, love.

A further study of the same song shows further examples of short rests, all of the greatest significance, which all too frequently are either ignored, or exaggerated for vulgar purposes of 'illustration'. '[S]iehe wie ich beb' und stöhne' (see how I tremble and sigh) is written: 'siehe [*rest*] wie ich beb' [*rest*] und stöhne'—two short moments of silence which express the overwhelming, almost unbearable intensity of the singer's feelings (see Ex. 10*b*). The feelings themselves are expressed in the underlying legato of the phrase, but when those two rests are ignored, the phrase becomes too bland. If, on the other hand, those two moments which, I suggest, should express the lover's sheer sense of wonder at the over-powering strength of his own feelings, are vulgarized into a sort of lustful panting (also too often heard), the whole essence of the song is spoiled.

All the above is an attempt to try and understand why the composer has written a few quaver rests.

There are many similar examples of such short silences carefully put in by the composer, and often ignored by singers too lazy to pay attention, too lacking in imagination to understand their significance, or so arrogant that they think they know better. There is a passage in Wolfram's Prize-Song in *Tannhäuser*, where the vocal line is broken by short rests, indicating, both the fact that Wolfram is improvising, and also the extreme importance to him of what he is saying—as though he were overwhelmed by the power and beauty of the emotions he feels towards Elizabeth (see Ex. 11). I recently heard this sung by a baritone so overwhelmed by the beauty of his own voice, and the efficiency of his own lungs, that he sang the whole phrase in one uninterrupted breath—thereby destroying the special atmosphere that Wagner had created, but attracting to himself much praise for his 'breath control'.

There is no necessity to take new breath every time there is a rest; some of the most expressive silences are those that are

Ex. 11. Wagner, Wolframs's Prize-Song, from *Tannhäuser*, Act 2

Wolfram

not used for the purpose of taking breath. In the example given above, only the second of the three rests should be used for that purpose; but that is no reason to ignore the moments of pregnant silence.

Such 'changes' to the written text do not provide evidence of singers' superior imagination; on the contrary, usually they demonstrate all too clearly their *lack* of true imagination, their lack of the ability to enter into the composer's mind.

It would be foolish to suggest that even the very greatest composers were incapable of miscalculation. But singers, as indeed any other performing musicians, must be quite sure that they have done everything within their powers to try to understand what a composer has written—even why the miscalculations were made—before making their own 'improvements'.

One of the greatest pleasures to be found in the preparation of any vocal music lies in the examination of small details, and in trying to imagine why the composer bothered to write them down. Such examination can sometimes completely change the approach to a passage.

In Schumann's song 'Waldesgespräch', at the end of the young knight's first section, Schumann writes a semiquaver rest into the phrase 'Du schöne Braut! ich führ [*rest*] dich Heim' (see Ex. 12*a*). This tiny rest, I suggest, introduces an element of frivolity into a passage which could too easily otherwise appear as a sincere and loving invitation.

Ex. 12. Schumann, 'Waldesgespräch', from *Liederkreis*, Op. 39

(a)   **Ziemlich rasch**

du   schö - ne Braut! ich führ' dich   heim!

(b)

der jun - - ge Leib, __   jetzt kenn' ich dich,

(c) 19

Trug _____ und

Later, as the young man piles on the specious compliments, he speaks of 'der junge Leib'—the young body. Schumann puts in a ritardando, dwelling on the word 'Leib'—a two-note ritardando, followed immediately by *a tempo* (see Ex. 12*b*). If Schumann's instructions are obeyed, it greatly increases the impression given that the young knight is only interested in the girl's body; and only then, as he reaches out to embrace it, does he realize that there is no body there for his reaching hand to grasp. He realizes suddenly that the girl is not human, but a spirit—the dreaded sorceress-seductress Loreley. If, as is so often the case, the singer makes a ritardando over the whole phrase, then the feeling of the whole section changes; the young knight again becomes almost too sincere; the song becomes sentimentalized.

And what of the Loreley? The strongest indication given as to how the singer should approach her music is given again in a tiny detail: the mordent written on the word 'Trug' (Ex. 12*c*), and again on the words 'gebrochen', 'her', and 'kennst'. If that mordent—a cold shiver—is sung instead as a softening appoggiatura, as is often the case (because the mordent is difficult to execute), that momentary *frisson* of cold danger provided by the mordent is missing. The singer will be tempted to interpret the girl's music as being softly, warmly, feminine, vulnerable, and full of feeling, instead of being the music of a beautiful but cold and destructive spirit, lacking in genuine human emotion. The Loreley reveals herself as a dangerous threat in that tiny detail. Once this is realized, then the singer must sing the whole passage in a different way—beautiful but cold—whether the actual mordent is consciously heard as such or not. If the significance of that tiny detail is missed, then the danger of sentimentalizing the song becomes much greater.

Remember Clara Schumann's remark:

> Play what is written; play it *as* it is written. It all stands there. . . . My husband's music is full of sentiment, but is *never sentimental*.

The apparent sentimentality associated with some of Schumann's music is almost always a result of performers ignoring Clara's advice.

Details which are all too frequently ignored, but which require special attention are:

1. *Up-beats*—long or short. Incorrect up-beats, or incorrect anacruses, almost invariably indicate that the singer has not made the intake of breath an integral part of the musical phrase, which as a result very often partakes of the wrong character. Remember: The character of a phrase is determined by the first note, and the character of the first note is determined by the anacrusis.

2. *The length of final notes*. Very often the composer makes a modulation in the harmony of the accompaniment during the last note of a singer's phrase. The effect of this modulation can be destroyed if the singer shortens that note. Also, holding on to the last note for too long can completely change the effect of an accompaniment, particularly if the accompanying postlude involves an harmonic modulation, a new thought, or a change of feeling. Benjamin Britten invented a new musical notation, which he called the 'Curlew sign', because he first used it in his opera *The Curlew River*:

(⌢). It means: hang on to the note until you sense the new harmony, and then let it go.

3. *Rhythmic detail*—particularly when this is unexpected, and is designed by the composer as a 'special effect' of emphasis.

4. *Rests.* The singer should be quite clear about the difference between expressive rests within a musical phrase—which often should not be taken as an opportunity for breathing (at most they should be associated with a top-up breath—certainly not a full breath) and rests which separate phrases, or introduce new thoughts or feelings, involving new anacruses, and usually a new main breath.

5. *Syncopation.* This is usually introduced as a means of momentary reinforcement of energy, and should not be ignored or glossed over. (See Ex. 13.)

6. *Moments of harmonic tension*, which need not be exaggerated or emphasized, but which are too often 'softened' by singers. All they need to do is to be acutely aware of the accompaniment and the harmonic implication of what they are singing.

It is not only in the song repertoire that composers write a lot of detail. A glance at almost any page of an opera by

Ex. 13. Richard Strauss, 'Zueignung', Op. 10 No. 1

Mozart, Verdi, Wagner, Puccini, or Britten, for example, would reveal considerable care taken with the smallest detail—every one giving some meaningful indication of the composer's thoughts and intentions.

But I must repeat: the purpose of this concern with detail, during the study of vocal music, is not the details themselves, but the key they can give to the composer's intention for the whole. Having been worked on with the imagination, details must be absorbed into the singer's unconscious mind, and the song approached 'in large'. The words and the music must become the singer's own, but should, of course, coincide with what the poet and the composer have written.

If singers react to the text and the music, rather than to the situation which gave rise to them, they put themselves at one remove from the source of the inspiration, and their performance becomes a description, or a commentary—in the worst cases a caricature—rather than a living performance. They must always sing as though text and tune came from their own imagination.

Colour

To recapitulate what I explained in the chapter 'Colour': The three main adjustments which the singer must make in order to sing with appropriate tone-colour are:

1. *Quality.* With the exception of songs where the singer is called upon to portray more than one character, the voice quality should remain constant throughout a song.

2. *Mood.* Mood can change within a song, but in general these changes occur between phrases or paragraphs; the mood can change with changing thoughts or feelings—but not normally from word to word. Excessively rapid changes of mood are usually indications of serious mental disturbance, and if indulged in by singers out of a misguided desire to be 'interesting', can produce a very false impression, and cause great unease and irritation in an audience, and can seriously interfere with, or even destroy, the overall effect of the music. As Reynaldo Hahn has written:

When we pronounce a phrase or a succession of phrases, we may remain in the same spiritual state, for generally our frame of mind, our mood, does not change with extreme rapidity.

3. *Verbal colours.* Words on the other hand, expressing thoughts, can change with great rapidity—in fact with 'the speed of thought'. But care must be taken, as always, not to confuse vowels of phonation (moods), and vowels of articulation.

Many songs, particularly in the German repertoire, are small-scale dramatic scenes. It is usually comparatively easy in such cases to know who is singing. The singer must *become* that person; must be able to distinguish between characterization, which comes from appropriate choice of voice character and mood, and mere caricature, usually produced by distortion of vowels of articulation (putting on funny voices).

The instances where different qualities are needed within a single song are mostly in songs where different characters are portrayed, songs like 'Vergebliches Ständchen' by Brahms, where alternate verses are sung by two different people, or of course Schubert's 'Erlkönig', where there are four characters: the narrator, the boy, the father, and the Erlkönig (I remember Gerald Moore suggesting that there are really five characters—the fifth being the horse, portrayed by the pianist, carrying the whole thing on his back, and keeping it moving!). Such songs are effectively mini-operas, and the approach must be dramatic. As explained above, the singer should *become* the characters, by changing both quality and mood. Attempts to 'characterize' them by 'imitating different voices' can reduce them to ridiculous caricatures.

In the case of 'Erlkönig', my suggestion would be:

1. If the singer is a man, the *narrator* is the singer himself, using the voice which is appropriate to his own character. He is the observer of an extraordinary and moving scene, but he does not need to characterize this part in any special way. The greater his detatchment, the more dramatic the effect. The same applies if the singer is a woman.

2. The *boy* is in a state of panic, desperate and emotionally overwrought. This needs voice quality approaching the dramatic. The high-lying phrases produce the necessary emotional tension. The combination of lyric-dramatic quality, fearful mood, high-lying pitch, and pianissimo can create an atmosphere which the often-heard attempts to caricature a boyish voice render impossible.

3. The *father* is concerned, progressively more and more worried, but does everything within his power to calm and reassure his son. He seems to be trying to be not emotional, but very calm. The combination of lyrical quality, fearful mood, and low-lying pitch achieves this perfectly. The artificially darkened tones so often assumed by singers can simply turn the father from a deeply troubled man into a pompous 'father' stereotype.

4. The *Erlkönig* is not human, and the more the singer can eschew voice qualities expressing human feelings the better. This means a move towards light voice quality, a rather neutral mood, beautiful but cold—instrumental. It is the lack of human warmth, coupled with clear enunciation of the insinuating words, that makes the Erlkönig so frightening— not the exaggerated spookiness sometimes heard.

Hugo Wolf's song 'Herr, was trägt der Boden hier', from the *Spanisches Liederbuch*—surely one of the most perfect songs ever written, because of its simplicity, its intensity, and its clarity—is a medieval poem of a conversation between the Christian Soul and Christ. Here we appear to have two characters, and the temptation for the singer is to change voice quality, rather than mood, with each half-verse. I have even heard this song performed as a duet—an act of artistic vandalism if ever I heard one. The point here is that the 'Christ' in this poem is not someone 'out there', it is the inner Christ. This song is not an extroverted conversation between two people, it is a spiritual meditation; an inner conversation between two aspects of one person, the Christian pilgrim. The two parts of the song require very different moods—the troubled soul, and the calm, loving, accepting Christ-figure—two aspects of the same character. Two utterly contrasting moods; but change of basic voice quality and character would be quite inappropriate. The song is a meditation, not a strip cartoon. (See Ex. 14.)

It is not, however, my intention to provide answers; rather to suggest what questions need answering. For singers with imagination, the composer will have suggested answers to all these questions, and many more, and will have incorporated those answers into the music, either consciously or intuitively. Singers must first decide what the possible answers to these questions may be, and, with the music and their own intuition and imagination to guide them, must discover what they can about the composer's indicated intentions. All these answers influence the way in which the song is sung. They influence the singer's posture, and facial expression; they influence the degree and type of energy brought to the singing. They tell the singer how to sing.

After all this work, I suggest most strongly that singers should spend time playing with the song. Having absorbed all aspects that require study and preparation, they should give themselves the pleasure of letting their imagination run riot, of fooling about with the song—sending it up, even—having fun with the song, and treating it as if it were entirely their own, before returning to the discipline of the composer's text. Unless singers can maintain the feeling of sheer joy in the act of singing, maintain contact with their *impulse*, they will not find the energy which is essential for any performance. The hard, serious work should be in the preparation. If all the preparatory work has been absorbed into the subconscious, then the actual performance should be fun. Singers should have the feeling that they themselves are both poet and composer. If the preparation has been thorough, and if, through the imagination, contact has been established with the source of the song's inspiration, then the performance can be given the spontaneity that it needs. They will then be re-creating the song, which 'happens' to coincide with what the composer has written, and will be able to bring to it their own creative

Ex. 14. Wolf, 'Herr, was trägt der Boden hier', from *Spanisches Liederbuch*

Ex. 14. *Continued*

Dor - nen, lie - bes Herz, - für mich,

und für dich der Blu - men Zier."

energy. They will be able to switch on their magnetism, and will be able to establish a magical connection with the audience, who will be able to share their experience of the poet's and the composer's inspiration. But all this can only come about if all the preliminary spade-work has been done, and the results thoroughly absorbed into the singer's subconscious. Every performance can then have the quality of a true improvisation. But improvisation as a replacement for complete and serious preparation is never more than the resort of a lazy and dishonest singer.

One of the important lessons to learn from all the above is

that a great deal of a singer's work—in terms of time, mental effort, and imagination—can, and should, be done silently. Simply singing a song repeatedly, without the necessary preparation or concentration, can be seriously counter-productive, as well as being vocally enervating. With proper preparation though, the singer will be amazed to discover how quickly, and how freely, his vocal apparatus can adjust to what is required of it. Most singers spend too much time singing aloud (or rather, making aimless vocal noises, in the hope that it will eventually come right) and far too little time in preparation, singing silently in their imagination.

I cannot overemphasize my advice to young singers to follow the method of Caruso and many of the great singers: not to work vocally on their songs until both words and music resonate clearly in their minds. I return to the maxim of Arthur Cranmer: 'Never allow a sound to come out of your mouth until it has passed through your mind.' Good, sound, practical advice.

Or as Lamperti wrote: 'When you are sentient from head to foot *and know your song*, you are ready to sing. Until silence is pregnant with the tone urgent to be born, you are only making vocal noises.'

Legato and Tessitura

Legato

In the first edition of *Groves Dictionary*, H. C. Deacon writes: 'Instrumental music gets its legato, and the more subtle parts of its phrasing from the singer.'

Instrumentalists and conductors frequently use the word 'sing' to describe a true legato. In fact 'singing' and 'legato' are to a very large extent synonymous, as Richard Wagner clearly thought, when he wrote: 'To play an instrument correctly means to *sing* with it.'

It is perhaps worth considering for a moment what is meant by 'legato'. Literally, the word means 'bound'. In a musical context, it is generally taken to mean that a phrase is 'performed with a smooth connection between the notes' (Scholes). That is all well and good, but if that is all that is implied by the word, then I am at a loss to understand why Deacon should have chosen singing as the source of true legato, rather than, say, the clarinet.

Clearly he was implying something more; some characteristic inherent in good singing, in addition to the 'smooth connection', which instrumentalists strive to emulate. That characteristic, I suggest, depends on the unique ability of the human voice to include not only the notes, the pitch, the two-dimensional aspect of the vocal line, but also a third dimension: harmony. A legato phrase is indeed 'bound'; by continuity of the spectrum of harmonics; by continuity of timbre, that timbre including all aspects of vocal colour, in particular the internal harmonic dimension.

Without this strong feeling for tonality, combined with a securely established *intention*, the true singer's legato loses its harmonic dimension, and becomes simply a two-dimensional 'smooth connection'.

Some years ago I was travelling by train, and fell into

conversation with a man who turned out to be a musician (unfortunately I have forgotten his name). His profession had been to teach musical theory to student instrumentalists and singers. I suggested, rather disloyally, that teaching harmony to young singers might not be an altogether easy task. His reply interested me greatly: 'On the contrary. I find in general that it is rather easy to teach harmony to singers; often easier than with instrumentalists; so much so that I have come to believe that a well-developed sense of harmony is an important part of the talent for singing. I have never known a really good young singer who lacked it.'

Legato is best practised, and developed, by commencing with the shortest possible musical phrases. It involves one of the most fundamental of singing skills: the ability to think in terms of phrases rather than notes; to think ahead, to anticipate. Only with this mental skill is it possible to develop the physical habits which result in the necessary homogeneity of timbre in all its aspects, and true singing legato.

Exercises for the development of legato are many, and can be found in any book of solfeggi or vocalises. All I would add is that the best exercises are in the end useless unless they are linked to the singer's feelings and musical imagination. Therefore, as it is far easier to conceive of a musical phrase as whole if it is associated with words, well-chosen legato songs and arias are in general much to be preferred. As Sims Reeves wrote: 'The best vocalises for all singers will be found in Handel's oratorios. Practising the runs in 'Messiah' will develop flexibility in a voice much better than the vocalises in all the tutors' books ever published.'

As a first stage in acquiring this habit of singing phrases rather than notes, it is necessary to sense the vibration of every note before it is 'activated'. This applies both in the case of the first note of a phrase, and also in all subsequent notes. The singer must 'hear' the note in his imagination before it is sung.

Ida Franca, in her *Manual of Bel Canto* gives the graphic illustration shown in Ex. 15.

As Lamperti said: 'When the voice is irresistibly attracted

Ex. 15. Ida Franca, illustration of legato from *Manual of Bel Canto*

to the pitch of the next tone, you can sing;' or again: 'Prepare to sing each succeeding phrase while still on the one preceding it;' and 'To anticipate the "feel" of resonance before singing, and to keep the sensation during pauses and after singing, is the lost art of the Golden Age of Song;' and finally: 'Hear your song in advance as though text and tune came from your own imagination.'

Lilli Lehmann wrote: 'To me it is always as if the pitch of the highest tone were already contained in the lowest, so strongly concentrated upon the whole figure are my thoughts at the attack of a single tone.'

Before singing a legato phrase, singers should be able to sense a spectrum of vibration containing all the notes in that phrase, and then move within that spectrum. It is what I call 'giving each phrase an harmonic envelope'. This skill is achieved simply by singers training themselves to be at all times acutely aware of the harmonic context, and the harmonic implications of every phrase they sing; to be aware that the human voice is an harmonic, as well as a melodic, instrument.

It is reported of Rossini's tenor, the great Manuel del Populo Vicente García, that his teaching was to a very large extent based on improvisation. This was in order that the singers should at all times remain in touch with their musical imagination. My observation is that whenever singers are genuinely improvising—whenever they sing something which is directly connected to their imagination and feelings—however well or badly they 'produce their voices', they tend to sing legato.

Ernest Ansermet has pointed out that composers always compose tonally, unless they make a conscious decision not to do so. In the same way, singers when singing spontaneously, will always tend to sing tonally, and legato, unless they make a conscious decision, or have somehow been conditioned, to do otherwise. Someone singing in the bath or under the shower, unless obsessed with vocal mechanics, or simply making noises, will improvise, and sing, phrases rather than notes. They will express feelings, however crude or banal, and these feelings will express themselves through the language of feeling—harmony. They will therefore tend to sing with a feeling for the harmonic dimension, and will sing legato.

The ability to sing a complete legato phrase depends primarily then on singers' ability to imagine a phrase as a whole, rather than simply proceeding, however smoothly, from note to note as though each note were a separate entity; on their ability to relate the notes to each other, and to the tonality of the phrase—to give them an internal harmonic context. It is, like all aspects of singing, an activity first and foremost of the imagination, of musical, dramatic, and poetic awareness. It requires a great effort of concentration, both mental and physical, and endless practise. It requires of singers that they maintain unbroken, poise, alertness, mood, impulse, and intention. It demands that singers should be able to conceive of their song 'in large'; and although true legato permits the maximum flexibility and subtlety of surface detail, it can all too easily be destroyed by self-conscious overelaboration of that detail.

As Lucie Manén wrote in *The Art of Singing*, 'Before singing a phrase the singer must make an assessment of that phrase as a whole—where it starts, how it is shaped and where it leads to. Each phrase should therefore be seen as a complete unit like a word, and not just a sequence of single notes like letters forming a word.'

Singers must be aware, whether consciously or intuitively, of which notes in any phrase are structural, background notes, and which are decorative, foreground notes. All vocal music should be based on an underlying legato, the basic adjustment of the voice following the harmonic structure of the music, whatever is happening in the decorative foreground.

It is, I believe, no accident, that the period in musical history when classical singing reached its high point, was the period, roughly from the beginning of the seventeenth to the end of the nineteenth centuries, when the harmonic aspect of music was most firmly and securely established. The two things were, I suggest, inseparable. Wagner, in his report to Ludwig II, on plans for a Bavarian state music school, insisted that all music students, including composers, should commence their studies with singing.

Tessitura

If, as I have suggested, legato is associated with the harmonic aspect of the singing voice, then it is important that its use should be as precise as possible.

The word 'tessitura' has in general lost some of its original meaning. Literally, it means 'texture'. It has come to be used to describe simply the general lie of the pitch of a particular phrase or song. Its original meaning in the context of singing was, I believe, more precise. It is associated with the specifically harmonic aspect of legato.

Harry Plunket Greene describes it as follows:

Every song feels to the singer to be upon a certain level, and to move forward in its straight line upon that level. . . . Songs have a mental as well as physical *tessitura* . . . both indicate a region in which the song should lie. The key to the mental *tessitura* is generally one note, round which all the other notes seem to group. . . . If [the singer] can once get the insistent call of it into his ears, it will have a direct physical result in the actual singing. He will find that not only will the song seem to be wound up and running like clockwork . . . , but that the sounds themselves will seem to come from one particular point in the actual sounding-board of his head, the point to which his 'poise' note called them.

Ex. 16. Lilli Lehmann, 'The Great Scale', exercise from *How to Sing*

Rossini stressed the importance of 'homogeneity of timbre' as being a *sine qua non* of good singing. Lilli Lehmann writes of an exercise which she calls 'The Big Scale' as being the most valuable of all singing exercises. She recommends it as a daily practice for all professional singers. It is the simplest exercise for legato and tessitura (see Ex. 16). The essentials of this exercise—which is far from easy to perform well—are:

1. Complete homogeneity of tone-colour.
2. That the repeated fifth and octave in particular should be sung with the same tone-colour (particularly harmonic) as the first fifth and octave.

In this case the tessitura note, which should be held in mind throughout, is the lower C.

Of this exercise, Lilli Lehmann writes: 'It equalises the voice, makes it flexible and noble, gives strength to all the weak places, operates to repair all faults and breaks that exist, and controls the voice to the very heart. Nothing escapes it. . . . In my opinion it is the ideal exercise, but the most difficult one I know.' All this is very true, but Lilli Lehmann omits the most important aspect of the exercise. She writes of the great scale as though it were purely a physical exercise. In fact this exercise is above all an exercise in concentration, and that is why it is so difficult!

Rossini, remembering his days as a singing teacher, as reported by Edmond Michotte, gave an example of the exercises he had used to achieve this homogeneity of timbre, 'Thanks to which I obtained astonishing results. It is simple, and the pupil himself, given a good ear, came to be able to correct himself'. (See Ex. 17*a*.) A simple version of the same exercise is given in Ex. 17*b*.

Ex. 17. Rossini, exercise for achieving homogeneity of timbre and tessitura, showing first half on low tessitura (C natural) and second half with tessitura an octave higher: (*a*) original exercise; (*b*) simpler version

The point of both these exercises is that all the notes of an octave scale are sung, while holding in mind first the lower tonic as the tessitura note—the 'sea-level'—and then the upper tonic note. In fact, the high octave, sung from the low tessitura, actually feels as if it is an octave lower than the same note as sung from the high tessitura.

Establishing the tessitura or sea-level of every phrase, is an essential element of true legato, and also of the harmonic tension-relaxation, which is one of the principal features of all music, and which, I venture to say, stems originally from

the experience of vocal modification—singing. All parts of the
phrase which are above this sea-level seem to have a down-
ward pull. All notes below it an upward pull. Often, but by
no means always, the phrase actually ends at sea-level, in
which case, there is a distinct feeling of home-coming at the
end of the phrase, or perhaps at the end of the song; whenever
sea-level is reached.

When a singer has developed a sense for tessitura singing,
it is as if there is no longer any feeling of 'up and down'; every
phrase becomes horizontal in feeling, with greater or less
harmonic tension as the melody procedes. The voice moves,
as it were, within a continuous spectrum of harmonics, the
tessitura note of each phrase providing its centre of gravity.

It is perhaps significant that at a time like the present, when
harmony and tonality in music have become subservient in
importance to pitch, we tend to hear more and more singing
of doubtful intonation. When singers come to think of singing
as merely 'producing vocal noises with pitch', it is perhaps no
wonder. Pitch, in singing, without context, or a strong sense
of implied harmony, frequently appears to be out of tune. I
recall a colleague commenting on a singer whom we had just
heard vocalizing his way through an opera. 'He is not actually
singing out of tune; it just *sounds* out of tune.' I refer you also
to the chapter 'The Pitch-Intensity Effect,' above.

I well remember leaving, early, a recital by a world-famous
soprano, because her out-of-tune singing actually made me
feel nervous. As I left, a colleague accosted me. 'Surely you're
not leaving?' I replied that I could not stand the out-of-tune
singing. He answered 'Oh, I know she does sing out of tune,
but what a wonderful voice!' A wonderful instrument may
be, but nothing could persuade me that she was a great singer.
(I subsequently heard a broadcast of part of a master-class
given by that same singer, in which she told her students that
they should think of each note as a completely separate entity.
A recipe, if ever I heard one, for vocal self-indulgence, and
unmusical singing!)

An example of the importance of sensing the tessitura can
be found in the 'Agnus Dei' of Britten's *War Requiem*. Here

there is the constant pull towards the lower F sharp; the initial high F sharp must be sung with the lower F sharp firmly in mind. Sung 'two-dimensionally' or with the tessitura centred on the upper F sharp instead of the lower, the song becomes rather bland, and sweetly cosy. The 'Pacem' becomes the peace which is the absence of struggle, of tension, instead of a peace which is longed for in the midst of struggle. (See Ex. 18.)

Let me give some more examples of the effects of finding the right tessitura. First two songs from Schubert's song-cycle *Die schöne Müllerin*.

'Morgengrüss' is a direct personal greeting to the loved one. The tessitura lies in this case around the fifth—the low fifth, on which the song begins. The low tessitura gives the song its direct, uncomplicated, almost earthy quality. The tessitura is centred around the lower G natural. (See Ex. 19.)

Immediately after comes an altogether more ethereal and poetic song, 'Des Müllers Blumen'. The young miller imagines that the flowers will speak for him to his beloved. Here the tessitura is the tonic, and the legato is achieved by keeping in mind the tonic note (E natural) in the upper part of the spectrum. (See Ex. 20.)

The actual *range* of these songs is more or less the same. The tessituras are widely different, as are the moods of the two songs.

Ex. 18. Britten, 'Agnus Dei' from *War Requiem*

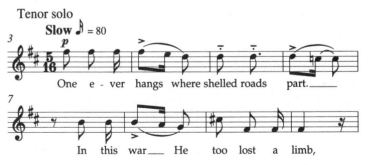

Ex. 19. Schubert, 'Morgengrüss', from *Die schöne Müllerin*, D795

Look at the first song of Schubert's *Winterreise*. The first sentence is 'Fremd bin ich eingezogen' (as a stranger I arrived). If, as is usually the case, the first phrase is sung smoothly and blandly—instrumentally—there is no dramatic tension. If on the other hand the singer is aware that the tessitura note is the *low* tonic (D natural), and that the first note is consciously sung as a tenth of that low tessitura note, which is held in the mind throughout the phrase, then the word 'Fremd' (foreign) has all the tension that Schubert clearly intended—without the singer having recourse to exaggerated verbal effects. The tension in that note, and the progressive relaxation as the phrase settles down to its low tessitura sea-level, is, or should be, produced entirely through awareness of the harmonic content. (See Ex. 21.)

A properly developed head-voice is essential to proper

Ex. 20. Schubert, 'Des Müllers Blumen', from *Die schöne Müllerin*, D795

Ex. 21. Schubert, 'Gute Nacht', from *Die Winterreise*, D911

tessitura singing. In the case of the high tessitura, it is the 'silver thread above the voice' of which singers speak; a high 'drone', from which the phrase is suspended. With a low tessitura there is a continuous 'drone' in the lower part of the harmonic spectrum, while the melodic movement is performed with the upper part of the spectrum.

A good example is Susanna's fourth-act aria in *Le nozze di Figaro*. If, as I believe is right, the first phrase is sung with the final F in the mind from the very beginning (low tessitura) the whole character of the aria is different—more deeply felt and sincere—than if, as one so often hears, the initial C is taken as the tessitura note. In the latter case, the aria becomes

Ex. 22. Mozart, 'Deh vieni non tardar', from *Le nozze di Figaro*, Act 4

Sussanna

Deh, vie - ni, non tar - dar, o gio - ja bel - la.

altogether more superficial, more flippant. (Some directors seem to require this—I believe they are wrong.) (See Ex. 22.)

Other examples are to be found in the two arias of Zerlina in *Don Giovanni*. (It is remarkable, how often one's mind turns to Mozart or Handel for examples of clear understanding of singing. Wagner, in his plan for a music-school for Munich, even attributes much of the superiority of Mozart's symphonies to the '*singing* character of his instrumental themes'.)

In her first-act aria, 'Batti, Batti', Zerlina is simply trying to wriggle out of a difficult situation. She tells Masetto 'hit me, for being a naughty girl!'. She is being grossly flirtatious. This is best achieved by thinking of the high F as the tessitura note; the note which is continually calling throughout the aria. To think of the lower F as the tessitura note would give the aria an altogether too sincere and serious a feeling. (See Ex. 23.)

Ex. 23. Mozart, 'Batti, batti', from *Don Giovanni*, Act 1

Zerlina

Bat - ti, bat - ti,o bel Ma - set - to, la tua

po - ve - ra Zer - li - na: sta - rò qui come agnel -

-li - na le tue bot-te ad a - spet - tar,

Ex. 24. Mozart, 'Vedrai carino', from *Don Giovanni*, Act 2

In the second-act aria, the situation is quite different; it has become much more serious. Masetto has been beaten up and seriously hurt by Don Giovanni as a result of Zerlina's irresponsible behaviour. She is genuinely contrite, and shows her real concern and affection for Masetto. Here the tessitura note is the low C. This gives an altogether deeper feeling to the aria. It has nothing to do with singing more heavily or more darkly. It is simply that there is a deeper harmonic content, expressing deeper and truer feelings. (See Ex. 24.)

Imagine Leonora's aria 'Pace mio Dio' from Verdi's *La Forza del Destino* being sung with a high tessitura! It would sound quite ridiculous. (I have heard it, and it did!) Leonora is praying for peace from the very bottom of her heart—and from the bottom of her voice. The opening phrases, starting on the high F must be sung with the low octave B flat as the tessitura. The first note is sung as a twelfth of that low B flat, with the phrase settling to a mere octave. The desperation in Leonora's voice comes from singing the high opening notes from the lowest possible tessitura. (If this very low tessitura is felt to create too desperate a feeling, then the low F could be chosen instead.) (See Ex. 25.)

The examples I could give are endless, because what I have written applies to every phrase of every song written by

Ex. 25. Verdi, 'Pace mio dio', from *La forza del destino*, Act 4

Leonora

composers possessing an instinct for vocal writing. It is also the reason why singers, called upon to sing atonal music, usually try to find an imaginary underlying tonality for each phrase. It is the only way in which it is possible to sing such music with a true singing legato, and to avoid its degenerating into simply a series of unrelated vocal noises.

Awareness of the tessitura, and the harmonic texture of the vocal line, is an essential element in the art of transforming a series of notes into sung musical phrases, binding them together into an harmonic envelope of true legato. It is a major element in avoiding that type of singing described by Plunket Greene as 'all over the shop'; that distressing habit, so often heard from those who concentrate on one note at a time, of singing as if each note were a separate entity, sometimes even as though being produced by different singers. Such awareness is one of the essentials of good singing.

Pulse

Music do I hear?
Ha! Ha! keep time:—How sour sweet music is,
When time is broke, and no proportion kept!

(Shakespeare, *King Richard II*, V. v. 41–3)

In his famous book *Interpretation in Song* (1912), Harry Plunket Greene writes:

There are certain rules which apply to every song in existence. They must have been so assimilated into the singer's very being as to be forgotten in detail and to become unconscious in their application. Their observance is not only due to the song in music, but is essential to successful performance, for they are intimately associated with the knowledge that *singer and audience sing, in reality, together in sympathy* [My italics]. There are three main rules—few but comprehensive—and of these the first is *musically* far the most important, for it is the mainspring of all singing, from a phrase to a song-cycle.

Plunket Greene's 'Main Rule 1' is: Never stop the *march* of a song.

Although I do not intend to quote him at length, I freely acknowledge my indebtedness to his book, on this, and indeed on many other, aspects of the art of interpretation. After all, although I am writing nearly a century later, and although styles of performance have changed, the qualities that are basic to all musical performance have not changed. The aspects of performance which change are a matter of fashion, and are largely superficial. The aspects which speak directly to our instincts and our feelings remain constant. The danger inherent in much modern concern with so-called 'authenticity' in performance practice, is that exaggerated concern with superficial aspects of musical performance—fashion—can easily deflect performers from the musical and poetic essentials. In particular it can too easily lead them to forget that their prime purpose is to communicate the contents of whatever it is that they are playing or singing.

One of the strongest reasons for the power that music has over us is the sympathetic response of the audience to the living musical pulse felt by the performer. This is true of all music; but because singing provides the most direct connecting link between music and human feelings, with singing it becomes especially apparent.

Reynaldo Hahn writes:

Nothing is more depressing or irritating than listening to singing without rhythm. This is like walking on uneven ground . . . in the end, one judges that it is simply not worth the effort to follow the singer into this rough terrain where he moves in no clear direction . . . By contrast, nothing gives a greater sense of security, of vigor and ease, than truly rhythmical singing where everything falls into place . . . There can be no musical delight without rhythm, without cadence, without that pleasant, periodic surge that regulates all the movements of nature.

All music worth the name has, like any warm-blooded creature, a pulse. A man or a woman without a pulse is, quite simply, dead. Anyone with an erratic pulse is sick. A man or woman with a pulse which is unvarying and mechanical is not able to respond physically to the varying energetic and emotional demands which life presents. This applies equally to music. A wrong note can often go unnoticed. A lapse of memory is quickly forgiven and forgotten. A failure in the ongoing pulse of the music interrupts the sympathetic contact between performer and listener; quite simply, it kills the music.

The onward march of a song must be flexible; the stride will lengthen and shorten, will quicken or slow down, but it must never stop; the singer must never get out of step with the music. There can of course be pauses, but these pauses should never interrupt the forward impulse of the music. Pauses and moments of silence must always be pregnant with meaning, and with the singer's ongoing intention. The inner pulse must never be allowed to stop or flag; concentration and intention must never be permitted to waver. A song, an aria, or a recitative must always push on, thought by thought, note by note, word by word, phrase by phrase, paragraph by paragraph, from its initial up-beat to its inevitable end.

This means that singers must train themselves to be able to visualize that inevitable end. They must know where they are going, and they must know how they plan to get there; by a gentle stroll, a steady march, a dance, a sprint, or a mixture of all these. But whatever character of pulse is appropriate to the particular music, even if that character changes during the journey, and even if there are moments of silence on the way, singers must never lose sight of the destination if the audience is to be taken along with them. If they pause, they must never lose concentration; they must mentally sing through the rests; they must not stumble, or simply stop for any extraneous or uncontrolled reason.

Some of these extraneous reasons are: simple lapse of concentration; overelaboration of detail; pauses for cheap effect; exaggerated obsession with voice and with the mechanics of vocalization; lack of a sense of rhythm; interruption of the rhythmic impulse in order to take in breath.

This last is one of the most common causes of failure in the musical pulse. The usual chain of events is something along these lines:

1. The singer runs out of breath.
2. The instrument is dropped, the chest allowed to collapse, concentration and musical intention are lost.
3. A large breath is taken, the singer tries to recover form, and finally:
4. Starts to sing again.

The vision of where the music is leading has been lost (assuming it had been there in the first place); the singer's attention has, momentarily, become entirely concerned with filling the lungs. If, on the other hand, physical and mental concentration and buoyant poise are maintained, together with the ongoing feeling for the pulse of the music, then replenishment of breath should be entirely automatic, a response to the musical impulse; it should never, and need never, become a preoccupation.

Every time a singer drops this state of alert concentration, every time the sight of the musical destination, and feeling for the pulse of the music, is lost, for whatever cause, then contact with the audience on the direct, instinctive level is also lost. The audience may well continue to listen; if the interruption occurs because of overelaboration of detail, or superimposition of inappropriate detail, they may even say to themselves: 'Oh! how clever' ; and the critic who has already heard too much music that week, and was gently nodding off to sleep, will, jolted back to wakefulness, perhaps write an admiring notice. But the singer will have lost contact with the responsive members of the audience who were 'singing along', who were sharing the singer's, the composer's, and the poet's vision and experience. Every time singers disobey this rule, for whatever reason, the magnetic thread which binds them to the audience will be broken.

It is here of course that the accompanist or the conductor must share responsibility with the singer. It is usually their lot to establish the tempo and the pulse of the song, to establish the atmosphere, and to provide the singer with an up-beat in character with the music.

Singers must feel the pulse from the up-beat to the first phrase of the accompaniment. They must not simply wait and listen while the accompanist plays the opening bars, waiting to join in when their turn comes. Singer and accompanist or conductor must breathe together from the very beginning of the song. The accompanist must never cause the singer to trip up; should never interrupt the flow of the song for a purely pianistic effect, like a suddenly delayed accent, or an arbitrary pause as hands are lifted off the keyboard with a gesture which, whatever spurious so-called artistic reasons given for such musical bad manners, in fact simply means 'to hell with the composer, to hell with the singer; listen to me'. (Yes, accompanists too can sometimes suffer from the effects of self-consciousness and inflated feelings of self-importance!)

Singer and accompanist or conductor must share the same vision of the music. Then the first thing that must be established is a shared feeling for the ongoing pulse, and for the anacrusis. Unless they breathe together, this sharing is not possible. This is even more important than establishing the 'correct tempo'; tempo and pulse are not the same thing. Tempo can vary, within reason, from day to day. But the feeling for the pulse of the music must always be there, and always related to the pulse of the text. Only when this is strongly established is it possible to have the freedom to make the subtle, spontaneous rhythmic variations known as rubato. Without a strongly felt pulse, rhythmic variations simply interrupt the flow of the music and irritate the listener.

It is important to distinguish between the living, flexible pulse, and the rhythmic 'beat', which is concerned with the smallest time-values of the music. There are indeed cases where the accompanying figure of a song provides a regular steady beat, while the vocal line has a pulse of far greater rhythmic flexibility.

The pulse of a song is almost always slower than the rhythmic beat. It is much more related to what Ernest Ansermet calls 'cadential rhythm'—the strong feeling for the music's progression from cadence to cadence, rather than from barline to barline; it is inseparable from a strong sense of phrasing, and line. It demands that the singer should be able to think ahead, have a clear picture of where the weight of a phrase lies, be able to move towards that point, and then to move on.

In his Meyer Lecture, given at the British Institute of Recorded Sound in 1963, Ernest Ansermet pointed out that all musical rhythms are founded on the two basic rhythms of human existence. Our respiratory cadences which, when no exterior influence alters their regularity are: binary (♩/♩), which we adopt when we are active, (for example, in marching), and ternary (♩/♩), which we spontaneously produce when at rest. As Ansermet has written, 'Musical rhythm is not founded on the smallest time-value, as too many contemporary composers believe; it is not made of time-values which may be added to one another; it is made of binary and ternary rhythmic cadences. . . . which are linked to one another in continuous movement.'

This feeling for the cadential pulse of the music is essential, particularly for singers, for whom rhythmic pulse and breathing are most essentially and intimately linked. The consequences can sometimes be surprising, as for example in Brahms's well-known song 'Sapphische Ode' (see Ex. 26).

The song is written alla breve, with slow-moving bass accompaniment, and with gentle syncopation for the accompanist's right hand. Too often one hears the singer moving, one note at a time, as if in a 4/4 rhythm, with periodic interruptions for breath and disturbing rallentandos interrupting the flow of the song. Alternatively it is sung with a strong two beats in a bar, which tends to make the syncopated movement of the accompaniment sound restless. When considered from the point of view of the cadential pulse of the song, the rhythm of the vocal line ceases to be binary, but ternary, with three-bar phrases, one slow beat to the bar, and the weight of the phrase on the third beat (the first beat of every third bar, as written). This enables the singer to forget the barlines, and to create the feeling of tranquillity that the song requires. The syncopated accompaniment which so often sounds restless, can then actually enhance the feeling of tranquillity by a gentle movement which helps to avoid any stress on the strong beats of the bar. The last two bars of each verse retain the ternary character, although doubling the speed of the pulse, and bring the verse to a clear and positive conclusion.

If the singer has a strong physical feeling for the slow *ternary* pulse of the song, and a clear mental picture of the shape of the phrases, then it will be found that the long breaths are no longer a problem. The song can flow peacefully to its final cadence.

There are many examples of songs where the pulse of the vocal line is quite different from the *apparent* pulse of the accompaniment. Méphistophélès's serenade in Berlioz's *Damnation de Faust* is an example that springs to mind. Here the accompanying figure is an ongoing, regular, energetic 3/4 Tempo di Valse (see Ex. 27a), while the vocal line has a rhythmic pulse, which, growing out of the words, always moving forwards, impelled by the almost relentless energizing

Ex. 26. Brahms, 'Sapphische Ode', Op. 94 No. 4

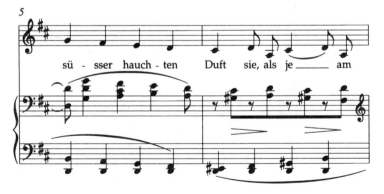

Ex. 26. *Continued*

Ex. 27. Berlioz, serenade of Méphistophélès, from *Le Damnation de Faust*: (*a*) figure of orchestral accompaniment

accompaniment, is constantly varying in its accentuation. The song varies between one beat every three bars, one beat every two bars, one beat every bar, and, for the penultimate bar of each verse, three beats to the bar; all arising from the free accentuation of the text, which, I suggest, can vary from performance to performance (see Ex. 27*b*). Giving the vocal line of this miraculously subtle song the same regular *one*-two-three beat as the accompaniment would reduce a serenade of infinite wit, charm, and character, to a rather commonplace ditty.

It is a useful general rule that one should find as slow a pulse as possible, whatever the actual tempo, for any song, particularly in the vocal line. The slower the pulse, the greater the freedom for possible rubato within that pulse. But that freedom should never disturb the strong feeling for the on-going movement, the cadential pulse, the structure of the music, and the underlying legato which is at the root of all good singing (yes! even in the case of quick, staccato songs).

Ex. 27(*b*). verse 1

Mèphistophélès

Finally, I make no apology for repeating yet again: the pulse of the song must be felt before the song begins, and then initiated by the up-beat, the anacrusis, the singer's preparatory gesture. The appropriate silent intake of breath, and the focusing on the mood, the intention, and the ongoing pulse must, as always, be stimulated by, in character with, and an integral part of, the song which is to be sung.

PART IV

Performance

This last part of my book is by far the shortest, but also possibly the most important. It is shortest because it is concerned with what must be entirely personal to each individual singer, and cannot therefore be categorized. It is most important, because the whole of the art of public singing, the art of the interpretation of vocal music, is concerned with communication; communication of the thoughts and feelings of the poet and the composer to a listening audience. (I am not speaking here about the spontaneous, artless, private singing of someone working in their garden, or going for a country walk; of someone singing to keep their spirits up or simply to express personal feelings of well-being.) The public singer's function is not only to experience and to give expression to thoughts and feelings, but to share them in such a way as to involve the audience: 'To purge men of their passions not by soothing them, but by arousing in them those very passions' (Galliver). This should never be forgotten; everything that a singer does in the way of training and preparation should be undertaken with this aim in view, if the many pitfalls of self-consciousness and self-indulgence are to be avoided.

It is here that the growth of gramophone recording, particularly since the development of modern recording techniques, and the vast expansion of the recording industry, has most significantly changed the approach of singers to their art, and of audiences to their way of listening; changed, I believe, for the worse, in that it has encouraged a purely instrumental approach to singing, at the expense of character and individuality. Audiences seem to have come to look for impressive superficial perfection, something which they can admire, rather than something which moves them.

The use of the tape-recorder in singers' own studios, while being of great benefit if used with discretion—that is, used as a means of checking what has been done after the event—can, if overused as a 'sound mirror', make it all too easy for singers to get into the habit of listening to themselves sing from outside, and of striving to reproduce a preconceived sound rather than feeling themselves sing from within; of increasing self-consciousness, at the expense of self-awareness.

Whereas in its early days, recording was simply a record of established public performances, today, public performances have often taken second place to studio recording. Audiences attend concerts in order to see (often literally to see, rather than hear) artists whose records have impressed them. Members of the audience at public concerts have, in the process, been to a large extent relegated to the role of observers, or eavesdroppers, rather than participants. One result of this is that singers too often tend to look on members of the audience as critics—there to observe and judge—rather than as fellow human-beings with whom they have something that they wish to share.

Electronic amplification has tended to diminish the necessity for the singer's own ability to project. In opera-houses, the use of surtitles, however useful, has recently gone one step further in distancing performers from the audience, of deflecting singers' direct lines of communication with the listeners, and also of encouraging them to neglect the essential elements of diction and declamation.

Techniques of studio-editing have led to concern, amounting to obsession, with the search for superficial perfection. Singers are too often encouraged to adapt themselves to the microphone, instead of recording techniques being adapted to the singer. It is a rare singer indeed who is capable of establishing, with a microphone, the magnetic thread of shared experience that should be an essential element in every performance.

This magnetic thread is not a one-way energy flow; as a shared experience, it involves both performer and listener, and therefore can affect the performance in subtle but very significant ways.

It should be perfectly possible for singers, in a studio, to share their experience with an *imagined* audience. But the moment this imagined audience is forgotten, an essential element in the singer's performance disappears. It ceases to be a 'live' performance, and however superficially and technically perfect the recording may be, however much energy is poured into the performance, it is almost certain to lose some of its true vitality and spontaneity. We forget Darwin's principle: 'The effect [of a song] is seen to depend not merely on the actual sounds, but also in part on the nature of the action which produces the sounds.'

In any performance we have:

1. Composer/Poet, and the source of their inspiration;
2. Singer, and accompanying musicians;
3. Audience.

Our concern must be with singers, and their relationship with the other two. So far in this book I have been primarily concerned with singers' relationship with the composer and the poet, and through them with the source of their inspiration. If the singer is to give a true, interesting, and even, possibly, inspired performance, this relationship must be closely studied, and the results of that study absorbed by the singer.

The other part of the relationship—that between singer and audience—is also an essential part of the singer's purpose of interpretation. In his book *Interpretation in Song*, Harry Plunket Greene writes:

Any singer who has sincerity, a fair amount of imagination and perfected technique can interpret, but not necessarily successfully. To be successful he must have Magnetism . . . Magnetism is the indefinable *something* which passes from singer to audience and audience to singer alike, for the audience which the singer holds in the hollow of his hand, holds him as surely in its own. Each acts and reacts on the other in ever-increasing degree. It is a gossamer thread over which passes that nameless electric current which stirs the singer to his depths and holds his audience thrilled and still.

Esther Salaman quotes Franklyn Kelsey: 'Make your audience come to you: never go to your audience. *You* are the magnet: the audience is that which is drawn into the magnet. Never reverse your proper role. This is the inmost secret of all great performance.'

Magnetism is a gift. It is perhaps the greatest gift that a singer can have. If it is there, and for any reason has been suppressed, it can be released, and enhanced; but it is something entirely personal and individual. Nothing is more embarrassing to an audience than a singer, lacking magnetism, trying to imitate the manner, or mannerisms, of those who have such a gift. These habits can only lead to an increase in self-consciousness, and as such are always counter-productive.

It is to a very large extent a question of mental attitude, the genuine wish—need—to share. It begins as soon as the singer prepares to walk on to the stage, and is established most strongly during the moment of silent, concentrated, anticipation, before starting to sing. The timing of that moment of silence is something which cannot be calculated; only a strongly developed performing instinct, an intensely felt need to share something with the audience, can help.

Singers remember: audiences are there to enjoy themselves, to enjoy the music and the poetry, through your singing. They are not there primarily to criticize; it is a sort of insult to them to behave as though they were.

The factors which most interfere with the working of magnetism are:

1. *Self-consciousness, and self-absorption.* This leads to affectation, and includes excessive concern with the mechanics of singing, which can result from either inadequate technique (technique which has not become second nature), or from the habit of mind—vocal vanity—which believes 'voice' *per se* to be all that matters. It is also frequently the result of singers' absorption in what they have just sung, rather than total concern with what they are about to sing. Whether the backwards look is admiring or hypercritical, it is equally destructive. The 'critic sitting on the left shoulder' has destroyed many a singer's performance. Singers must learn to be self-critical, but at the moment of singing, they must function as performers, not as critics. By the time a phrase has been sung, it is too late to do anything about it. Singers, like any performing musicians, must always be looking forwards, always totally involved in what they are about to sing—in their intention. They must register what they have been doing

(for future consideration and work), but must never allow concern with what is past to deflect their ability to react, and their concentration on what is to come. Closely linked to this is:

2. *Lack of preparation*, be it musical or technical preparation. And directly related to this:

3. *Lack of concentration on the work in hand*. If preparation is adequate, if technique and ability to 'switch on' energy and singing impulse has become second nature, then singers should be able to concentrate entirely on the musical, dramatic, and poetic *content* of what is being sung. Only then is it possible for them to be open and responsive to the poet's and the composer's source of inspiration, and to become the vehicle for the song's spiritual content.

4. *The wish to importune*—to make an impression on the audience. This is an aspect of self-consciousness, a one-way directing of energy which tends, at a deep level, to set up resistance—to repel rather than to attract the audience.

Factors which encourage magnetism are:

1. *Physical and mental poise*, which can only come as a result of good postural habits and technical security.

2. *Thorough preparation* (like Callas, know your score).

3. *Concentration, and anticipation*—letting the imagination lead, and re-creating the song at every performance, rather than just repeating it. The memory must be an indispensable and obedient servant; but singers must not become its slaves.

4. *Sharing*. The mental attitude of wishing to share your experience of the poetry, the drama, and the music, with the audience, and to establish a relationship with the audience by drawing them towards you. Closely associated with this is perhaps the most important of all: sheer joy in the act of singing and sharing. 'Never sing until you feel that you would die if you didn't.'

Richard Wagner considered what he called *Das mimische Wesen*—best translated as 'the performing instinct'—to be the essential basis of all performance. He writes: 'The art of sublime illusion . . . does not come from any form of lying; this is what divides the genuine performing artist from the bad comedian whom present taste delights to load with gold and laurels.' (Things have not changed all that much!)

I have to admit that there are many honest, competent, worthy, singers who lack the quality of magnetism—and there are mountebanks who have it in abundant measure. One can only encourage the former to develop and improve their ability to communicate—perhaps they may be helped by some of the hints in this book—and the latter somehow to acquire more artistic integrity.

If a two-way flow of magnetism is to be established, singers must be open in their attitude to the audience; and this, of necessity, implies the acceptance of a high degree of vulnerability. These feelings of vulnerability can be distressing to singers of sensitivity, and can only be dealt with by being physically and psychologically well centred and well grounded, thoroughly well prepared, and aware. If these feelings of vulnerability are resisted, then members of the audience will sense it, and will feel themselves, in a subtle way, to be either rejected, or put upon; they will sense that they are reduced to being mere observers rather than participants, and they respond, at a deep level, by setting up a spiritual barrier between themselves and the singer, even though, at a more superficial level, they may be full of admiration for what is being done.

Singers must, in effect, in the moment of performing, be able to love the audience, and must genuinely wish to share with them the experience, through singing, of the poet's and the composer's inspiration. I do not mean the sickly sentimental declarations of 'love' on the part of some popular performers, whose actual performance belies every word they have spoken. I must also emphasize here the words 'in the moment of performing'. What singers feel about their audience for the rest of the time, when not singing, is entirely their own affair!

Establishing magnetic lines of communication is in many ways easier on the operatic stage than on the concert platform; and this is particularly so in the case of duet scenes. It is easier, in an operatic role, for singers to immerse themselves in the character they are playing. Two singers performing together can establish a strong magnetic relationship, which can (and should) be extended to include the public. (The danger here is that the relationship between the singers can become so intense that the public is forgotten—excluded.) The audience in such scenes tends to identify with the one who is being addressed, who should listen with at least the same degree of concentration as that used by the active singer. Many of the most dramatically successful and powerfully affecting scenes in opera are between two people. Think of Violetta and Germont in *La Traviata*; King Philip and Rodrigo in *Don Carlos*; Rigoletto and Gilda in *Rigoletto*; Rudolfo and Mimì in *La Boheme*; Hans Sachs and Stolzing, or Eva, or Beckmesser, in *Die Meistersinger von Nürnberg*; Falstaff and Ford, or Alice, or Mistress Quickly in *Falstaff*; and so on *ad infinitum*. (Mozart's long finales are often to a large extent a series of duet scenes, in the sense that the character who is singing is more often than not addressing another particular character—rather than making a general statement.) In all these scenes, the existence of the listening partner is all-important in establishing the lines of communication between singer and audience.

Such scenes have another advantage for singers. Good singing, like all good dramatic performance, is not only a question of *acting* but of *reacting*. If the partner being addressed really listens in a concentrated, alert way (I exclude here the self-conscious 'acted' listening, where the singer sends semaphore messages to the audience: 'look at me, I'm listening') then the singing partner will have something clear to which he or she can react, as can the listening partner, when the time comes for them to sing; for both partners the anacrusis is thus made easier.

In the case of operatic soliloquies, or song recitals, singers must provide their own anacrusis; they must *react* entirely to what is happening in their own imagination. I remember a young singing student, an excellent singer with a strong natural dramatic talent, expressing this very clearly to me, when he said: 'I don't think I am really yet capable of performing songs, or even solo arias; without a partner, I find it is so difficult to know what to react to.'

Some singers deal with this by reacting to the music that they are singing, instead of re-creating it; this puts them at one remove from the source of inspiration. Instead of conveying to the audience the thoughts and feelings of poet and composer, with imagination and freedom of expression, all they succeed in doing is to communicate their own feelings about the music and the poetry. They tell the audience how much they personally enjoy the music, how 'musical' and 'artistic', how 'sensitive' they consider themselves to be, how beautiful they consider their voices. This is the ultimate counter-productive, self-indulgent, all-too-common example of singers' self-consciousness. It is the opposite of the complete absorption in the work, the complete identification with the character, combined with the wish to share, that should be their aim.

Such singers are demonstrating their self-consciousness and egotism; they are patronizing the poet and the composer, rather than seeking to relive their experience, and sharing it with the audience. As Harry Plunket Greene wrote:

The self-conscious singer cannot forget his *Technique*; he cannot forget his details—his mind cannot travel far enough away.

He cannot forget himself; he cannot, therefore, give and receive *Magnetism*.

He cannot visualise; he cannot let his imagination run; he cannot, therefore, feel *Atmosphere*; he cannot find the *Mood*.

His voice cannot *unconsciously* respond to the play of feeling; he cannot therefore, paint in *Tone-Colour*.

He cannot think of his song in large; he cannot therefore have *Style*.'

Such singers may well be capable of efficient vocalization, which can even, for a short time, be very exciting; they may impress with superficial virtuosity; but if singing is the interpretation of vocal music, then they cannot sing.

All the above observations apply equally to conductors and accompanists. Self-conscious accompanists can, by drawing attention to themselves with superfluous pianistic effects, or attempts to dominate the performance, deflect the lines of magnetic communication between singer and audience. They can destroy a song just as easily as can a self-absorbed singer.

There is one further thing I would like to say about the relationship between singers and their accompanists. In former times, singers were always advised not to use the same pianist as both coach and accompanist. Singers usually need the services of a coach to help them in the study of their music. This is, of necessity, a teacher–pupil relationship. If this relationship is then carried on to the concert platform, it cannot but act as an inhibiting factor in the singer's relationship with the public, by tending to deflect and dilute the 'gossamer thread' of magnetism. Singer and accompanist are of course partners in their performance, and I am certainly the last person to undervalue the collaboration of a fine accompanist. But singers must remember that it is they who are facing the audience, and establishing the lines of magnetic communication, and it is they who have responsibility for the imaginative declamation of the text. Singers and accompanists must be intimate collaborators in the performance of the songs, but the singer must always lead, and must be permitted to lead. If they are, even slightly, unconsciously seeking the approval of a pianist who has taught them the song, then their lines of communication with the audience are deflected. The performance is diluted. The old tradition, that the roles of coach and accompanist should be kept strictly apart, is one that should not be ignored.

There are some conductors who are adored by singers, because they feel supported and inspired by them; there are also conductors, sometimes famous and successful, who by continually dominating, instead of leading, and helping in the process of sharing, are positively hated by singers, who find it difficult to give of their best under their direction. I remember singing in a long series of performances of Mozart's *Così fan tutte*, shared by two conductors, one an experienced Italian opera conductor, the other an efficiently schooled young German. At that time my wife and I lived on the third floor of an apartment block. One evening, my wife said: 'I can always tell, when you come home, who has conducted *Così*. When the old Italian conducts, you run upstairs. When the other one conducts you walk up slowly, as though you are very tired.' She was right. The explanation was very simple. The old Italian breathed with the singers, and gave clear, energizing up-beats, and had a wonderful feeling for the pulse of the music, which he shared with the singers. The young man never breathed with us, and tried to 'drive' the opera and to dominate the singers, almost entirely with strong down-beats.

During the course of a music summer-school where we were both teaching, a great Hungarian conductor once asked me: 'What do you consider to be an operatic conductor's first and most important duty?' I replied: 'To breathe with the music, and with the singers, and to give clear up-beats.' His response was: 'You are right—that should surely be the duty of all conductors at all times.'

One of the great temptations that singers—indeed all musicians—have to face, is a result of giving many performances of the same work. Consciously or unconsciously singers can begin to indulge in irrelevant overelaboration of detail. I can here do no better than to quote Harry Plunket Greene again. Writing of unconscious overelaboration of detail, he writes:

This comes far oftener from over-familiarity than from deliberate intention. The mind and ear become so accustomed to the work that, if the performance is not to grow purely mechanical, new readings must be given to detail; the individual phrases are over-emphasised or distorted, the natural proportions are lost, the work loses its balance and the sense of style disappears. *The performer does it to satisfy himself not his audience* [*my italics*], but the effect is the same—you cannot see the wood for the trees.

A great deal of this book has been concerned with the singer's responsibility to the composer. Without performance, the composer's work is largely wasted, so perhaps it is not out of place for me here to ask that composers should have an equal feeling of responsibility towards singers, and that they should bear in mind Richard Wagner's statement that I quoted in my Introduction.

> The human voice is the practical foundation of music, and however far the latter may progress upon the path of its choice, the boldest expressions of the composer or the most daring bravura of the instrumental virtuoso must always return to the essence of song for its ultimate vindication.

It is sad that many singers today avoid the performance of much contemporary music. They do this, not necessarily because they are lazy or old-fashioned, but out of sheer self-protection. If composers write music which causes singers to risk losing their ability to sing the music for which they have trained, they have only themselves to blame if singers resist.

This situation is surely unnecessary. The human voice has within the limits of the traditions of classical singing an immense range of expressive possibilities. By ignoring these possibilities, and these limits, composers are denying themselves wonderful opportunities for musical expressiveness, and at the same time antagonizing many of the most well-intentioned, and accomplished, singers.

Perhaps I can sum up much that I have written by another quotation from Wagner's essay 'Actors and Singers'. He is writing about the dramatic soprano Wilhelmine Schröder-Devrient.

> Concerning this artist I have again and again been asked if her *voice* was really so remarkable, since we glorified her as a singer—the voice being all folk think about in such a case. It constantly annoyed me to answer this question, for I revolted against the thought of the great tragedian being thrown into one bevy with the female castrati of our Opera. Were it asked once more today, I should answer somewhat as follows:—No! She had no 'voice' at all; but she knew how to use her breath so beautifully, and to let a true womanly soul stream forth in such wondrous sounds, that we never thought of voice . . . ! Moreover, she had the gift of teaching a composer how to compose, to be worth the pains of such a woman's 'singing'. . . . all my knowledge of the art of performance I owe to this grand woman; and through that teaching can I point to *truthfulness* as that art's foundation.

Finally, I make no apology for repeating that the greatest enemy of interpretation is self-consciousness in all its forms. And perhaps the greatest cause of self-consciousness among singers is obsession with voice, and the practice of divorcing what is called 'technique' from what is called 'interpretation', and forgetting the sheer joy in singing; of failing to put into practice the principle that all singing, in all its aspects, physical, emotional, and spiritual, must be initiated in the singer's imagination.

For true singing artists, when the moment of performance arrives, the act of singing should be an act of faith. They should be able to trust all the work they have done in preparation, to activate the imagination, to open the spirit to the possibility of inspiration, and sing from the heart.

Bibliography

ANSERMET, ERNEST, 'The Crisis in Contemporary Music' (lecture), *Journal of the British Institute of Recorded Sound*, 13 (1964), 165–75.

AVERINO, OLGA, *Principles and Art of Singing* (Aarhus, 1988).

BENNATI, FRANCESCO, *Recherches sur le mécanisme de la voix humaine* (Paris 1832).

BUSTI, ALESSANDRO, *Studio di canto: Metodi classici del Conservatorio Reale di Napoli* (Naples, 1865).

CACCINI, GIULIO, Preface to *Le nuove musiche* (Florence 1602), ed. H. Wiley Hitchcock (Madison, Wisc., 1970).

CALZABIGI, RANIERI DE', Letter to Count Kaunitz, *Musikologie* (Praha-Brno), 1938, trans. Hammelmann and Rose, in 'New Light on Calzabigi and Gluck', *Musical Times*, 110 (1969).

CARUSO, ENRICO, *How to Sing* (London, n.d.).

CATHCART, GEORGE C., *Voice Production*, ed. Arthur Latham and T. Crisp English (private publication, n.d.), repr. from *A System of Treatment*.

DARWIN, CHARLES, *The Expression of the Emotions in Man and Animals* (New York 1872; repr. Chicago, 1965).

DAVIES, ROBERTSON, *A Mixture of Frailties* (1958; repr. Harmondsworth, 1980).

DEACON, H. C., Article on 'Voice', in *Groves Dictionary of Music and Musicians* (London, 1890).

DRYDEN, JOHN, Preface to Henry Purcell's *The Prophetess* (1690).

DÜRCKHEIM, KARLFRIED, GRAF VON, *Hara: The Vital Centre of Man* (London, 1962).

FRANCA, IDA, *Manual of Bel Canto* (New York, 1959).

FRY, PROF. D. B., and MANÉN, LUCIE, *Basis for the Acoustical Study of Singing* (London, 1957), repr. from *Journal of the Acoustical Society of America*, 29/6 (1957), 690–2.

GALLIVER, PROF. D., 'The Vocal-Technique of Caccini', *Poesia e musica nell' estetica del XVI e XVII secolo* (Florence 1967), 7–16.

GARCÍA, MANUEL, JUN., *Hints on Singing* (London, 1894).

HAHN, REYNALDO, *Du chant* (Paris, 1957), trans. Leopold Simoneau as *On Singers and Singing* (Portland, Oreg., 1990).

KAGEN, SERGIUS, *On Studying Singing* (New York, 1950).

LAMPERTI, GIOVANNI BATTISTA, *Vocal Wisdom*, transcribed William Earl Brown (Boston, 1931).

LEHMANN, LILLI, *Meine Gesangskunst* (Berlin, 1902), trans. R. Aldrich as *How to Sing* (New York, 1902; revd. edn. 1914).

LEVIK, SERGEI, *The Levik Memoirs: An Opera Singer's Notes*, trans. Edward Morgan (East Barnet, 1995), from the 2nd revd. Russian edn. (Moscow, 1962).

LUNN, CHARLES, *The Voice* (London, 1904).

MANÉN, LUCIE, *Bel Canto* (Oxford, 1987).

——*The Art of Singing* (London, 1974).

MANCINI, GIAMBATTISTA, *Pensieri e riflessione practiche sopra il canto figurato* (Vienna, 1774), trans. Edward Foreman as *Practical Reflections on Figured Singing* (Champaign, Ill., 1967).

MARTIENSSEN-LOHMANN, FRANZISKA, *Der Wissende Sänger* (Zurich 1956)

MESSCHAERT, JOHANNES, *Eine Gesangsstunde*, ed. Franziska Martienssen (Mainz, 1927).

MICHOTTE, EDMOND, *An Evening at Rossini's in Beau-Sejour (Passy)*, trans. Herbert Weinstock (Chicago, 1968).

NAVA, GAETANO, *Metodo pratico di vocalizzazione* (Milan, n.d.), trans. as *A Practical Method of Vocalisation* (London, 1891).

PLUNKET GREENE, HARRY, *Interpretation in Song* (London, 1912).

RAMACHARAKA, YOGI, *The Hindu-Yogi Science of Breath* (Romford, 1960).

REEVES, SIMS, *The Art of Singing* (London, 1900).

SALAMAN, ESTHER, *Unlocking your Voice* (London, 1989).

SANTLEY, SIR CHARLES, *The Art of Singing and Vocal Declamation* (London, 1908).

SCHEIDEMANTEL, KARL, *Voice Culture* (Leipzig, 1910).

SCHMIDINGER, JOSEF, *Biodynamische Stimmbildung* (Vienna, 1984).

SCHOLES, PERCY C., Article on 'Legato', in *The Oxford Companion to Music* (Oxford, 1938).

SHERWOOD, DR M. P., *The Back and Beyond* (London, 1992).

STEVENS, S. S., and DAVIS, HALLOWELL, *Hearing: Its Psychology and Physiology* (New York, 1938).

SPENCER, HERBERT, 'The Origin and Function of Music', in *Essays, Scientific, Political, and Speculative* (London, 1858).

TOSI, PIER FRANCESCO, *Opinioni de' cantori antichi e moderni* (Bologna, 1723) trans. Mr Galliard as *Observations on the Florid Song* (London, 1743).

WAGNER, RICHARD, 'About Conducting', 'A Music School for Munich', 'Actors and Singers', articles in *Richard Wagner's Prose Works*, trans. William Ashton Ellis (London, 1896).

Index